Isla

Islam

An Introduction to Religion, Culture, and History

James A. Beverley

THOMAS NELSON
Since 1798

NASHVILLE   DALLAS   MEXICO CITY   RIO DE JANEIRO

To my brother Bob Beverley
With much love and admiration

© 2011 by James A. Beverley

Published in Nashville, Tennessee, by Thomas Nelson. Thomas Nelson is a registered trademark of Thomas Nelson, Inc.

Book design and composition by Upper Case Textual Services, Lawrence, Massachusetts.

Thomas Nelson, Inc., titles may be purchased in bulk for educational, business, fund-raising, or sales promotional use. For information, please e-mail SpecialMarkets@ThomasNelson.com.

Library of Congress Cataloging-in-Publication data is available. ISBN 0-7852-4897-8

978-1-4185-4595-6 Paperback

Printed in the United States of America

11 12 13 14 15 RRD 6 5 4 3 2 1

Contents

Preface to the Second Edition   vii

Preface to the First Edition   xi

1. Islam   1
2. Muhammad   11
3. Quran   21
4. Muslims   33
5. Women   51
6. Jihad, Terrorism, and September 11   63
7. Palestine   75
8. A Christian Response to Islam   87
9. Now What?   93

Appendix A: Key Dates   97

Glossary   105

Frequently Asked Questions About Islam   109

Bibliography and Additional Resources   113

Preface to the Second Edition

I wrote the final words of this preface on the day that President Hosni Mubarak announced his departure as the leader of Egypt. The peaceful revolution in Egypt, the largest of Arab nations, was an excellent context for completing this second edition of *Understanding Islam* now titled *Islam: An Introduction to Religion, Culture, and History*. The first edition was written in the shadow of 9/11 and that day of infamy created a very sober context for helping people to understand Islam.

Despite the evil of the terrorist attacks, there was worldwide optimism in the fall of 2001 that the deaths of the 9/11 victims (in New York, Washington, and a field in Pennsylvania) would lead to greater efforts at peace among nations and among religions. Scholars of Islam—both inside and outside the religion—went public in an effort to make a clear demarcation between militant Muslims who support terrorism and the majority of Muslims who do not. Various books, including this one, sought to adopt an irenic spirit in interpreting and analyzing Islam. This second edition adopts the same spirit but with less optimism about humanity's ability to live in peace.

The last decade has not been kind to peacemakers and those who seek justice in the human community. The war in Iraq did not go as planned. Tensions have increased in Afghanistan and Pakistan. On the latter fronts, Ahmed Rashid's recent work on these two countries is aptly titled: *Descent into Chaos*. The world has been stunned by major terrorist attacks in Bali (2002), Madrid (2004), London (2005), and Mumbai (2008). The Israeli-Palestinian conflict remains a worldwide concern. While things look brighter in Egypt and Sudan, conflicts simmer in Lebanon and Nigeria. A Florida pastor threatened a public burning of the Quran in 2010, creating an international storm. The U.S. remains roiled in debate about the proposal to build a mosque near Ground Zero.

So, in many ways the larger context for this book is more depressing now than in 2001. This means that the demand is greater for care in interpreting and understanding Islam, avoiding simplistic, trite, and misinformed analysis on tough and complex issues. Since 9/11 I have continued to study Islam and have had the opportunity to broaden my research through wider contact with Muslim leaders and scholars of Islam. On the latter, I would like to thank several intellectuals who have been of particular help in conversations: Patricia Crone (USA), Lutz Richter-Bernburg (Germany), Frank Peters (USA), Efraim Karsh (United Kingdom), Josef Van Ess (Germany), Christopher Tyerman (United Kingdom), Michael Cook (USA), and Andrew Rippin (Canada). As well, I owe a particular debt to Hans Küng, my former professor, who has been a model of courage and wisdom as he addresses the religions of the world as a Christian statesman and public intellectual.

The earlier preface includes some other important remarks about my approach to Islam. I will simply repeat here my willingness to be corrected if I have made errors of fact about the various controversial topics in this book. On issues of faith and overall perspective, I welcome dialogue. Three large aims have shaped this book. First, it is written to tell people what most Muslims believe about their religion, with attention to minority readings of Islam.

Second, I want to provide readers with various positions about the major topics addressed. Finally, I offer Christian analysis of Islam in general, Muhammad, the Quran, the Muslim world, women in Islam, jihad, terrorism, and the Israeli-Palestinian conflict.

Thanks to Heather McMurray, my editor at Thomas Nelson, for her encouragement in getting this new edition into existence. I am grateful to Ann Stocker and Brett Potter for help in proof-reading. I also appreciate Christian friends from various parts of the world who have helped me in understanding Islam: Jay Smith, Wafik Wahba, Andy Bannister, Bob Morris, Gordon Nickel, Rick Love, Chad Hillier, J. Gordon Melton, and Massimo Introvigne. Writing a preface also gives an opportunity to think about the family that shapes my life and work. So, once again, I am grateful for my twin brother Bob, who gets this book dedicated to him for a second time. I remain deeply thankful to God for my wife Gloria, our adult children Derek and Andrea, and our son-in-law Julien. And, it is a delight to note that since the first edition of this book was published, a granddaughter Dorothy arrived.

James A. Beverley
jamesbeverley@sympatico.ca
February 11, 2011

Preface to the First Edition

Most people don't spend a lot of time thinking about religions other than their own. The fact that Islam is the second largest religious movement in the world has been true for many years. Events in the fall of 2001, however, suddenly brought Islam to the attention of people around the world as never before. Who are these people, and what do they really believe? How are they connected to international terrorism?

Muslims in the United States and all over the globe have been placed on the defensive, called upon to explain the basis of their faith. The lack of information about their faith has raised suspicions. Many Muslims have been subjected to verbal and even physical assaults.

Today more than ever before in history there is a need and a demand for information about Islam—about its essential nature, its prophet, and its holy book (the Quran). People want to know what Islam really teaches about the role of women, about jihad and terrorism, and about the Palestinian question and their view of Israel. Getting the facts is essential in order for us to keep daily events in perspective.

My aim in this book is to provide accurate, objective, and fair information about all of these issues. *Understanding Islam* is meant to give readers the basic and most important facts and perspectives. Every chapter has been written with attention to the crucial literature and the leading experts on every topic. My aim has been to serve as a reliable and trustworthy guide to momentous and complex topics.

Though I am not a Muslim, I have made every effort to be fair to the Islamic faith, as well as attentive to the critical issues that are being raised about Islam. What I have written is based on years of research as a scholar of world religions. My understanding of Islam is rooted in face-to-face encounters with Muslims in the U.SA., Canada, India, Kenya, South Africa, and England. My knowledge and perspective is also rooted in learning from friends and colleagues who have spent years living in Muslim countries and under Islamic rule.

In a world in which each day raises new questions, this book seeks to provide some foundational answers. It is hoped that out of an enhanced understanding will come a greater ability to view events from a broader perspective. Since my presentation involves some controversial issues, I ask that my readers examine my book with patience and care. I will give serious attention to thoughtful criticisms.

I am grateful to my wife Gloria, our children, Derek and Andrea, and to our son-in-law Julien for their encouragement. Thanks to Annie McKeown and Rachel Collins for research assistance, and to Kevin Rische and Aaron Matthews for computer help. For comments on argument and perspective, I am grateful to Bob Beverley, Jay Smith, John Wilkinson, Larry Matthews, Donald Wiebe, Bob Morris, J. Gordon Melton, and Mitchell Bard. Thanks also to Wayne Kinde, Lee Hollaway, Teri Wilhelms, Barbara West, and Phil Stoner at Thomas Nelson.

James A. Beverley
October 22, 2001

Islam

The Nature of Islam

One out of every six people on earth is Muslim, a follower of Islam, the second largest religion in the world, next to Christianity. Islam has been a religious, cultural, and political force since the seventh century AD. Today it plays a dominant role in the Middle East and large sections of Africa and Asia.

The Four Foundations of Islam

As in all religions, Islam has a core, an essence, a sort of DNA that has defined the religion from the beginning. The best way to begin to grasp this basic and fundamental identity is to recognize four absolutely key realities in the faith of all Muslims. These keys to understanding the Muslim faith are the same for all groups within Islam.

Allah

What is absolutely primary in Islam is a total belief in Allah (the Arabic term for God that is also used by Arabic-speaking Jews and Christians), Muslims believe with conviction that there is one supreme creator, an infinite, eternal power who can do all things and knows all things.

According to Muslims, Allah is the perfect, wise, merciful, and just guide who holds all humans accountable for their deeds, both good and bad. All of this is captured in the first verses of the Quran (Koran is the former English term), the Muslim scripture. "In the name of Allah, Most Gracious, Most Merciful. Praise be to Allah, the Cherisher and Sustainer of the Worlds." (1:1–2). It continues: "Master of the Day of Judgment. You do we worship, and Your aid we seek. Show us the straight way" (1:4–6).

Muhammad

Muslims also believe that Allah has spoken to the world through Muhammad, the seal (final and greatest) Prophet. The vast majority of Muslims believe that Muhammad (who died in AD 632) was sinless. Every area of Islamic life is patterned after what Muhammad taught, what he did, how he dressed, how he responded to threats, and what he said had been revealed to him by Allah.

The reverence and adulation of Muhammad is hard to overstate, though Muslims do not believe he was divine. However, those who cast aspersions on the prophet are in extreme danger, as Salman Rushdie, the Indian-born Muslim, discovered when he wrote The Satanic Verses. The Iranian Ayatollah Khomeini issued a death order on him because he thought Rushdie had slandered Muhammad.

Quran

Further, the Quran is absolutely fundamental to all Muslims. This is the Holy Book. Muslims believe the Quran was revealed to Muhammad and is the literal, actual Word of Allah. It should be recited in Arabic, the original language, should be memorized and studied, but never questioned as an ultimate source of authority.

Islamic views on everything are determined by what the Quran says or by what can be deduced from its general teachings. Thus, polygamy is acceptable to Muslims because the Quran says so. Some Muslim's believe women must be veiled because of an interpretation of one passage that demands modesty. In some countries with Islamic law the hand of a thief is amputated because the Quran says this is to be the punishment. Muslims have certain views about Jesus because of teachings in the Quran.

Law

Islam is also a religion of law. While every faith has general principles, some groups like like Orthodox Judaism and Roman Catholicism have elaborate rules. In Islam, Shariah (SHAR rih ah) law extends to every area of life, including how Muslim nations are to obey God's will.

The history of Islamic jurisprudence is very long and complicated, especially after Islam experienced a serious division following the death of Muhammad. Basically, Islamic law is derived first from the Quran, and then from the example (sunnah) of Muhammad. When neither the Quran nor the Prophet's life and teachings speak directly on issues, most Muslim legal authorities depend on reason and consensus to formulate either new laws or judgments based on the massive codes of law given in the three centuries after Muhammad's death.

The scope of shariah law is amazing to most non-Muslims. Consider, for example, some of the matters addressed in Islamic Laws, written by Ayatullah al Uzama Sye Ali-al-Husaini Seestani, a famous judge in Iran. He provides rulings (known as *fatwas*) on thousands of topics, including: (1) what direction should be faced when using the bathroom, (2) when swallowing thick dust makes fasting void, and (3) how much is owed Allah in almsgiving if a Muslim owns sixty-one camels.

Sunni Schools of Law		
School	**Founder**	**% of Muslim world under school**
Hanafi	Imam Abu Hanifa (699–767 CE) from Iraq	45%
Shafi'i	Imam al Shafi'i (767–820 CE) from Medina	28%
Maliki	Imam Malik (711–795) CE from Medina	15%
Hanbali	Imam Ahmad bin Hanbal (780–855 CE) from Iraq	2%

The Five Pillars of Islam

Just as the Ten Commandments shape Judaism, the five pillars of Islam constitute core patterns of faith for most Muslims.

Confession

The primary pillar is a confession of faith known as the *shahadah*, which reads: "There is no God but Allah, and Muhammad is His prophet." Devout Muslims repeat this statement several times each day.

Prayer

The second pillar involves the discipline of prayer (*salat*) and the call for all Muslims to pray at five specific times every day, facing Mecca, the holiest city. In traditional Islamic cultures, the call to prayer, resounding from the minarets (towers) of the mosques (houses of worship), brings all other activity to a halt.

Giving

This third pillar is known as *zakat*. The *zakat* is collected by a few Muslim states, but most Muslims give through leaving money in the metal *zakat* box in their local mosque. The money is used to help the poor and for emergency situations. The *zakat* involves giving 2.5 percent of a Muslim's assets, but it is not charity since it is an obligatory act, one that is usually to be done in private.

Fasting

Muslims are to intensify their spiritual focus through the fourth pillar *sawm* (fasting), from sunup to sundown during the entire month of Ramadan (the ninth month in the Islamic calendar). Unless prohibited by poor health, Muslims are to abstain from all food, water, and sexual activity from sunrise to sunset during the month of Ramadan. The fast offers a time for spiritual reflection, repentance, and giving to the poor. The whole Quran is often recited in evening worship over the thirty-day period. Ramadan ends with a three-day feast.

Pilgrimage

The fifth pillar, known as the *hajj*, is the command for all able-bodied Muslims to make a pilgrimage to Mecca at least once in his or her lifetime. Every year 2 million Muslim pilgrims make their way to Mecca. Outside the city both men and women don simple white garments, and enter Mecca while reciting "Here I am at your service, O God, here I am!" They circle seven times around the Kaaba, the temple built by Abraham and Ishma'il. The pilgrims engage in a ritual of running between two mountains outside of Mecca, in memory of the plight of Hagar looking for food and water. Muslims also throw stones at a pillar that symbolizes Satan, and sacrifice animals in memory of the story of Abraham and Isaac.

Seven Other Major Beliefs

From the aforementioned, we know that all faithful Muslims believe that Allah is the one true God. They also want to emulate Muhammad, obey the Quran, pray, give financially, fast, take the pilgrim's journey to Mecca, and obey the law of God in all things. Beyond these overriding and paramount aspects of Islam, seven other fundamental beliefs help paint an accurate picture.

Islam has Existed Since Creation

Muslims believe that Islam began long before Muhammad. They assert that Islam started when God created Adam and Eve, and that Islam was the religion of faithful Jews and Christians. So, according to Islamic tradition, Moses was a Muslim, and Jesus was too. Younis Shaikh, who taught at a medical college in Pakistan, was arrested in October 2000 for allegedly saying that Muhammad's parents were not Muslims and that Muhammad did not become a Muslim until he was forty.

Humans Are Not Born Sinful

Though Muslim views are similar in some ways to Christian tradition, Muslims do not believe in original sin. This is the concept that all human beings are born with a sinful nature. Muslims do believe that Adam rebelled against God's law in the Garden of Eden, but there was no fall of the human race, as is taught by most Christian groups. Humans are frail and weak, prone to temptation, obviously, but not predisposed toward sin.

God is Sovereign

Muslims believe in the total sovereignty of God. Islam's emphasis on this belief cannot be overstressed. In parts of Afghanistan, goals in soccer games are celebrated by shouting "Allahu akbar" ("God is great"). When I visited Kenya in 1994, I saw a vivid display of Islamic trust in God as I visited a poor Muslim area. There, on top of the most meager little home you can imagine, the owner had a sign, bigger than his house, proclaiming his faith in the great Allah.

Everything is Predestined

Muslim theologians developed a very rigid doctrine of predestination out of the emphasis on Allah's total supremacy. If God is all knowing and all powerful, He must, in some sense, be responsible for everything. If nothing really deviates from His will, and He knows the future, everything must be predestined—or so it has been argued. Some analysts of Islamic culture believe that a sense of fatalism has emerged as a result of this Islamic preoccupation with predestination.

The Spiritual Realm is Vast

Islam also teaches that our universe is home to angels, devils and spirit-beings known as *jinns*. Islam shares with Christian tradition a belief in Satan or the supreme devil, an angel who chose to rebel against Allah. Muslims also believe in angels, disembodied spirits who obey God. The English term *genie* derives from Muslim stories about the jinn, supernatural entities who can do both good and evil.

There will be a Day of Judgment. Islam has very definite views about the Day of Judgment. At a time known only to Allah, the world will end. All humans will be judged by their deeds. Humans await either eternal punishment in the fires of hell or eternal bliss in heaven. Islam has no Catholic notion of purgatory, and virtually no openness to any idea that all humans will eventually reach paradise.

The Quran describes Hell explicitly:

Those who reject our Signs, We shall soon cast into the Fire: as often as their skins are roasted through, We shall change them for fresh skins, that they may taste the penalty: for God is Exalted in Power, Wise (4:56).

Heaven is the Home of the Righteous

Muslims believe that heaven is the eternal home of the righteous. It is described in the Quran as a wonderful garden paradise, an image especially appealing to Muslims used to the sands of the Arabian deserts. There will be no sin, no death, and no tears in heaven. There will be special reward for Muslim martyrs. A few famous verses in the Quran promise that faithful Muslim men will be rewarded by beautiful women when they enter paradise. For both men and women the Quran states that "the greatest bliss is the good pleasure of Allah" (9:72).

Jesus is a Muslim Prophet

Muslims claim that Jesus is a prophet of Islam. Given the bitter hostilities between Islamic and Christian empires in history, it is often assumed that Muslims have no interest in Jesus. While Muhammad is the chief prophet, Muslims also look to Jesus as a spiritual guide. Often when Muslims speak of Jesus, they will add the phrase "Peace Be Upon Him," just as they do when Muhammad's name is mentioned either vocally or in print. For short, in writing you will often see "Muhammad (PBUH)" or "Jesus (PBUH)." Muslims also believe that Jesus will return at the end of time to defeat the forces of the Anti-Christ.

There are significant differences between Muslim and Christian understandings of Jesus. This is most easily seen by a list of Muslim negative assertions about Christian views. For Islam, Jesus is not the Son of God and not an incarnation of God nor is Jesus divine. He did not die on the Cross at Calvary as a sacrifice for sin. He was not put in a tomb outside Jerusalem. The Christian story of Easter is not true, though Muslims do believe that Jesus went to heaven when He died years after attempts to have Him crucified failed.

Muslims do agree with Christianity on the following points: Jesus was born of the Virgin Mary, was a prophet of God, lived a holy life, taught with wisdom and love, and performed many miracles. Muslims also unite with Christian tradition in teaching that Jesus was persecuted for His faith, was opposed to idol worship (as most Jews would be), and is now in heaven.

2

Muhammad

The Prophet of Islam

Some histories regard Muhammad as the most significant person in human history. Though Christianity claims more believers, these historians believe Muhammad had a greater impact on history because of the breadth of Islamic political power, the depth and range of Islamic spirituality; and the way in which Islam brings its ideology to bear on every facet of life.

Whatever the merit of this judgment, anyone who reviews the history of the world since the seventh century can see the profound impact Muhammad made in his lifetime and since. Muslims believe, of course, that Muhammad is the Prophet, the final Messenger of Allah. Thus our understanding of Islam is intrinsically linked with our knowledge and assessment of its Prophet.

The Profile of a Prophet's Life

This profile is based on what most Muslims believe about Muhammad. Many scholars argue that the data about him comes too long after he died to provide historical certainty about his life. Muslims generally accept that he was born about AD 570. Muhammad's world was tribal Arabia, where people believed in many gods.

Muhammad: Key Dates

570 Birth in Mecca

575 After death of parents, Muhammad was raised by grandfather and uncle

595 Married Khadijah, a travel merchant

610 Claimed to have a mystical experience of divine revelations that would form the basis of the Qur'an

613 Began to preach monotheistic message, which led to his persecution

613 Muhammad added then deleted "Satanic verses" out of the Qur'an because of false revelation that said worship of three idols was acceptable

619 After the death of Khadijah, Muhammad married Sawdah, the first of many other wives

620 Muhammad was taken by the angel Gabriel to Jerusalem and ascended to seventh heaven on a ladder. This is known as the *miraj*.

622 Escaped to Medina to avoid persecution in Mecca

624 Muhammad defeated Meccan enemies at the Battle of Badr

627 Married Zaynab, his cousin, who was previously married to the Prophet's adopted son Zayd

627 Raided the Jewish clan of Qurayzah and ordered the death of hundreds of Jewish men

628 Signed a treaty with Meccan leaders at Hudaybiyyah

630 Conquered his enemies at Mecca and removed idols from the city

632 Death on June 8 after a period of ill health

Muhammad knew pain early in his life. By age six or so both his parents were dead. His mother died right after he was born, and his father died later. Muhammad's grandfather raised him for two years until his grandfather's death. An uncle then took care of Muhammad until he reached his teen years. Some scholars of religion speculate on how these early losses may have had an impact on Muhammad in terms of his later ideology and behavior.

A merchant named Khadijah came into Muhammad's life, and they were married in 595, when Muhammad was about twenty-five. Though Khadijah was considerably older, she bore him at least six children, and by all indications they had a loving marriage. Muhammad did not have other wives until after Khadijah's death in 619.

On the seventeenth night of the Arabic month Ramadan, 610, Muhammad's life changed forever, when he was on Mount Hira near Mecca. Muhammad claimed that the angel Gabriel visited him in a powerful, terrifying, and transforming encounter. According to the earliest documents, a shaken Muhammad returned home and turned to his wife for confirmation of his prophetic call.

Three years later Muhammad began to preach to his Meccan neighbors. His message of one God met fierce resistance. Arabs were polytheistic. Mecca's main shrine, the Kaaba, said to be built by Abraham, was home to many gods. Muhammad gained some converts immediately, one of the most famous being his friend Abu Bakr. His earliest followers came mainly from the poor clans of Mecca, drawn to Muhammad's message of social reform.

Muslims believe that on a night in 620, one year after the death of Muhammad's first wife, the angel Gabriel brought Muhammad to Jerusalem on the back of a heavenly horse named Buraq. Then, according to Muslim tradition, Muhammad ascended to the seventh heaven, on his way meeting Abraham, Moses, Jesus and other prophets. Muhammad then met God. Muslims believe that the Dome of the Rock in Jerusalem is built on the spot from which Muhammad ascended. This episode is known as the miraj and is said to be the subject of surah (chapter) 17:1 in the Quran.

Two years later, in 622, in year one of the Muslim calendar, Muhammad was forced to flee to Medina, about 250 miles north of Mecca. Then, for eight long and bitter years, the Prophet engaged in repeated military battles with his Meccan enemies. There were significant victories (most notably on March 15, 624, at Badr) and major setbacks (one being at Uhud just a year later).

By January 630, however, Muhammad triumphed, took control of Mecca, and destroyed the idols in the Kaaba. Medina continued to be his home base. He led military campaigns in northern Arabia, and returned to Mecca for a final pilgrimage in early 632. He was in poor health at the time, traveled back to Medina, and died on June 8 of that year, in the embrace of Aisha, one of his many wives.

Alfred North Whitehead once wrote that philosophy is one long footnote to Plato (see *Process and Reality*). Likewise, Islamic history is one long footnote to Muhammad. Thus, Muhammad's journey—in all of its detail, from the mode of his prayer life, to his treatment of Jews and Christians, to what he did in battle—is the example for all Muslims.

Muhammad's life must not be compartmentalized, as if his spiritual life was distinct from his family life, military career, political strategies, or economic views. For Muhammad these were part of a seamless whole. Islam continued this pattern by refusing to think that the religious and the secular should be divorced. Thus, for many Muslims the American model of the "separation of church and state" is unacceptable.

Historical Accuracy and Muhammad

As we will see in the next section, there is a wide range of opinion about what we can know about the historicity of sources about Muhammad's life. There are five major sources for historical analysis: (1) the Quran, (2) biographies of the prophet, (3) *hadith* (sayings of Muhammad), (4) *tafsir* (commentaries), and (5) *tarikh* (Muslim histories).

Of these, the study of the hadith represents one of the most fascinating aspects of Islamic history and religious life. Muslim scholars had to try and sort through thousands of traditions involving Muhammad in order to decide what reports were accurate. The most famous collection of what Muslims regard as authentic hadith was done by al-Bukhari (d. 870). This collection is particularly significant to Sunni Muslims who make up the largest grouping of Muslims. Shi'a Muslims have their own hadith collections.

Western scholars have been divided over the value of the hadith in terms of what we can know about Muhammad. The traditions obviously tell us what Muslims and others were saying about the Prophet, and that has an interest for its own sake. There is increasing skepticism among experts about the value of both the Quran and hadith for giving us trustworthy information about Muhammad.

There is much disagreement between the two ends of the spectrum—Muslim scholars who accept everything from the Quran and the hadith as historical and non-Muslim and Muslim historians who feel it is their responsibility to question the historical reliability of both sources. Accepting a particular saying or deed of Muhammad as historical is a separate issue from whether or not one accepts that Muhammad's teachings are from God or if Muhammad was the prophet of God.

Three Basic Views of Muhammad

That there is an extreme range in opinion about Muhammad should come as no surprise since disagreement has existed since he first proclaimed Islam as the true religion God gave to Adam and Eve. Many wars have been fought over his ideology, even among Muslims. In the Iran-Iraq conflict in the early 1980s, where millions

Miracle Stories About Muhammad

The Quran as perfect book proves Allah as author

Muhammad taken on supernatural trip to Jerusalem and heaven

Prophet splits the moon in two to prove Islam

Angel opens Prophet's chest and washes his heart

Prophet multiplies food to feed hungry disciples

Water supply flows through Prophet's fingers

Wolf praises Muhammad's ministry

Muhammad heals crying palm tree

3,000 angels help Muhammad in battle

Two trees move to provide privacy for Prophet

died, both countries claimed to have Muhammad on their side, much like Irish Catholics and Protestants asserted that Jesus is with them when they fought each other. Three distinct views cover the range of interpretation about the prophet.

Muhammad the Perfect Prophet of God

The first view of Muhammad's significance is a theologically conservative one. Traditional Muslims view Muhammad as the greatest person who has ever lived and as the model for God's will in every area of life, spiritual, political, moral, economic, and social.

One way to capture Muslim appreciation for Muhammad is to note how even Islamic philosophers will write about the details of daily life with reference to the example of the prophet. For example, al-Ghazali, one of Islam's greatest thinkers, gave instructions on the cutting of finger nails on the basis of traditions about how Muhammad cut his nails.

Out of this immense adulation of Muhammad comes an equal anger against any who are perceived as ridiculing the Prophet. For example, Ahmed Deedat, one of the most popular defenders of Islam, circulated a pamphlet against the novelist Salman Rushdie, called "How Rushdie Fooled the West." His conclusion about Rushdie speaks for itself: "Mired in misery, may all his filthy lucre choke in his throat, and may he die a coward's death, a hundred times a day, and eventually when death catches up with him, may he simmer in hell for all eternity!"

Muhammad The Great Man

A second assessment of Muhammad is one step removed from Islamic orthodoxy, though a major step. We move to those who have a high opinion of Muhammad but who do not accept that he is the prophet of God or that Islam is the one true religion. Thus, Alphonse de LaMartaine, writing in *A History of the Turks* (Paris, 1854), said:

> If greatness of purpose, smallness of means, and astonishing results are the three criteria of a human genius, who could dare compare any great man in history with Muhammad? The most famous men created arms, laws, and empires only. They founded, if anything at all, no more than material powers which often crumbled away before their eyes. This man moved not only armies, legislations, empires, peoples, dynasties, but millions of men in one-third of the then inhabited world; and more than that, he moved the altars, the gods, the religions, the ideas, the beliefs and the souls.

Hans Küng, a Roman Catholic, took up the question of Muhammad's status in his book *Christianity and the World Religions*. He presents seven parallels between Muhammad and the prophets of Israel, outlines the immense contribution of Muhammad, and concludes by citing Vatican II, where one of the documents states that the Catholic Church "also looks upon the Muslims with great respect: They worship the one true God who has spoken to man."

Küng, who does not believe that Muhammad was sinless or that Islam is the one true religion, then offers this assessment:

> In my opinion, that Church—and all the Christian Churches— must also 'look with great respect' upon the man whose name is omitted from the declaration out of embarrassment, although he alone led the Muslims to the worship of the one God, who spoke through him: Muhammad the Prophet.

Muhammad as Evil

The third view moves to a whole other realm, one in which Muhammad becomes the embodiment of evil. This tradition of contempt began in the early Middle Ages as Christian and Muslim armies fought from North Africa, across the Middle East, and into Europe. Many Christians, popes included, viewed the wars as the necessary struggle against the Antichrist himself—Muhammad.

Dante's Inferno puts the Islamic leader in the lower realms of hell. William E. Phipps, author of *Muhammad and Jesus*, describes Dante's vision of Muhammad's fate.

> There he receives everlastingly some of the worse punishment that hell has to offer. A gash from throat to anus causes his intestines to hang between his legs. Many of the damned are so horrified by the mutilated Muhammad spectacle that they forget momentarily their own torment.

Such diatribes against Muhammad continue from Dante through the Reformation period, culminating in Luther's invective, quoted by Phipps:

Should you be called a prophet, who were such an uncouth blockhead and ass? When the spirit of lies had taken possession of Muhammad, and the devil had murdered men's souls with his Quran and had destroyed the faith of Christians, he had to go on and take the sword and set about to murder their bodies.

Secular writers have dismissed Muhammad with less contempt, but their views follow the same pattern: Muhammad was ignorant, barbaric, and immoral. He was either a hypocrite or delusional, perhaps the victim of epileptic seizures, whose success with converts has more to do with promises of sexual reward, material gain, and the proverbial Islamic sword.

In the aftermath of September 11, 2001, some editorials in the secular press hinted at Muhammad's dark side, with subtle accusations that the terror that rained down on New York and Washington has its roots in the life and teaching of the Muslim prophet. They cite Muhammad's all-or-nothing mentality, his expansionist vision, his dictatorship, and, of course, his love for Jihad.

One interesting factor here is that human beings arrive at radically different views while dealing with the same person, the same documents, and the same history. One author finds Muhammad racist, lustful, and irrational. He argues that his views are based on a careful reading of the hadith material about Muhammad. Muslims read the same traditions and regard them as proof that Muhammad was sinless and the greatest person who has ever lived.

If we look at a particular issue in hadith interpretation, we discover that the debate is not usually over what this or that tradition states. Muslim scholars know very well what particular hadith is being used to justify each specific attack on Muhammad. The difference of opinion has to do with larger philosophical, religious, and psychological views that are brought to the given issue.

Take, for instance, the incredible accusation that Muhammad was a pedophile. It is hard to imagine a more explosive thing to say about a religious leader, or anyone for that matter. Some Muslim scholars may want this accuser to die, but they know that he is referring to an infamous episode in the prophet's life when he took a very young girl to be his wife.

How could any Muslim scholar defend this today? First, some would simply refuse to entertain any possibility that Muhammad could sin. "He is the Prophet (Peace Be Upon Him), he is sinless. I cannot question God's Apostle (Peace Be Upon Him)." A second tactic would be to explain the event by reference to different cultural norms in Muhammad's day. "Who are we to judge another culture and their norms in marriage and family life?"

Finally, other Muslim scholars might say that the Prophet is exempt from the moral standards that apply to normal humans.

> Allah, the Sovereign Lord, alone decides what is right. His ways are beyond our understanding. We must trust him no matter what. Allah, in his infinite wisdom, gave the young bride to Muhammad (Peace Be Upon Him). Allah knows what is best.

Another process is for Muslims to resist all accusations against Muhammad by a reflex action that finds refuge in the sacred and eternal truths given by Allah through His Prophet. The thought that these truths can be shaken is simply beyond the imagination of many Muslims. Then, out of this faith and certainty, comes the challenge to all non-Muslims to read the Quran and see for themselves that God has given His Word in miraculous form to a weary and skeptical world.

When Muhammad was alive, he met challenges concerning his credibility by pointing to what he regarded as the amazing revelation that had been given to him from God's angel. To Muslims, that book proves the truth of Islam. That book is the focus of our next chapter.

3

Quran

The Quran: the Muslim Holy Book

Yusaf Ali's English translation of the Quran runs to 597 pages in one paperback edition. That is one indication of the space taken up by the Quran's six thousand or so verses. There is nothing amazing about the size of the Quran. What is amazing is that many Muslims, including young boys and girls, have memorized the entire Quran, cover to cover, in Arabic.

This remarkable feat is an indication of the incredible stature of the Quran within the Muslim world. It is a sin for a Muslim to place any book or object on top of the Quran. Every debate in Islamic law is settled by what the Quran teaches. For example, Muslim scholars who have condemned the September 11, 2001, terrorist attack have done so on the basis of their belief that the Quran condemns such evil.

The Origin of the Quran

Muslims believe that the origin of the Quran lies with Allah (85:22). Then, when the time was right, according to the will of Allah, the angel Gabriel dictated the revelations to Muhammad.

Traditional View of the Compilation of the Quran

Stage One: Gabriel revealed the Quran to Muhammad

Stage Two: Muhammad recited revelations to followers which they wrote down

Stage Three: Death of Muhammad in 632

Stage Four: Abu Bakr, (first caliph 632–34) ordered Zayd bin Thabit to make complete collection of Quran

Stage Five: Abu Bakr's collection was given to Umar I (second caliph 634–44) and then to his daughter Hafsa (one of Muhammad's widows)

Stage Six: Uthman (third caliph 644–56) ordered Zayd to compare various collections and make final version of Quran.

Stage Seven: Uthman sent his codex to Mecca, Bazra, Kufa, and Damascus. Uthman then ordered Muslim leaders to destroy other versions of the Quran. The Kufan leader Abdallah bin Masud (d. 653) refused, and his codex, therefore, has some differences with the Uthmanic one.

The traditional view is challenged by various Western scholars of Islam, including Arthur Jeffery, John Wansbrough, John Burton, Angelika Neuwirth, Günter Lüling, Andrew Rippin, Gerd-R. Puin, H.C. Graf von Bothmer, Patricia Crone, and Christoph Luxenberg (a pseudonym). A few Muslim scholars have adopted non-traditional views of the Quran, most notably Nasr Abu Zaid, Mohammed Arkoun, and Taha Hussein. The dissenting views were the subject of Toby Lester's controversial article "What Is the Koran?" in *The Atlantic* (January 1999).

He recited the words to his wife and then to the small group that became his first followers. The earliest members not only memorized the unfolding contents but also started to write them down. After Muhammad died, a number of Muslim leaders formed the final edition of the Quran.

Most Muslims absolutely reject theories about its alleged human origins. Islam states quite plainly that the Quran has one author:

Allah. It is not Muhammad's book. It is not, they say, a human book. It is divine. To question the Quran is to risk eternal punishment. To obey it is to gain eternal life.

Many scholars believe that the Quran lacks historical reliability since it cannot be traced back to Muhammad. Muslims believe that the Quran is perfect and contains no errors. What Allah revealed to Muhammad was passed on faithfully by the Prophet, according to Muslim tradition, with one famous and startling exception. Early in his work as a prophet, Satan fooled Muhammad into thinking that true followers of Allah could worship three Arab deities. For a very brief period, one of the chapters of the Quran contained approval of such pagan worship.

As soon as Allah told Muhammad of the deception by Satan, the Prophet moved quickly to remove the offending passage. Ever since, these verses have been called "the Satanic verses." This episode in the life of the Prophet is mentioned in the Quran, in the hadith or traditions about the Prophet, and in countless books. It is from this incident that Salman Rushdie titled his controversial novel.

The Structure of the Quran

The Quran contains 114 surahs or chapters, and more than 6,000 verses. The surahs are arranged by size, with the shorter chapters near the end. It is generally believed that the later chapters were written first and belong to the period when the Prophet was in Medina. The longer chapters were written last and were revealed after the Prophet conquered Mecca.

The titles of the various chapters are based on some word or idea that appears in the chapter, though the titles do not usually suggest what is the main theme of the chapter, if there is one. Some Muslim scholars teach that there are hidden scientific truths and hidden mathematical wonders in the Quran. For example, one writer argues that the divine inspiration of the Quran is proven by the fact that the Arabic word for "Most Merciful" is used 114 times, which matches exactly the number of surahs of the Quran.

The Eight Major Themes of the Quran

Many first time readers of the Quran find it confusing. It does not seem orderly, as most Muslims will acknowledge. The text does not follow a narrative, and it is not written in a systematic fashion. The surahs are not arranged by content, and there is no single theme in most chapters. The best way to understand the Quran is to first grasp the major themes that it addresses on its pages.

Allah

The Quran is absolutely dominated by reference to God. Verse after verse, page after page, beginning to end, Allah is everything to the Quran. The word Allah appears over 2,500 times. Anyone who says that the Quran is mainly about something else has never read the Quran. It is a book saturated with references to God. Here are ten major things, in alphabetical order, that the Quran says about Allah.

Creator. Surah 6:101–102 states: "He created all things, and He hath full knowledge of all things. That is God, your Lord! there is no god but He, the Creator of all things." Another passage expresses it this way. "He is God, the Creator, the Evolver, the Bestower of Forms (or Colors). To Him belong the Most Beautiful Names: whatever is in the heavens and on earth, doth declare His Praises and Glory: and He is the Exalted in Might, the Wise" (59:24).

Eternal. "God! There is no god but He, the Living, the Self-subsisting, Eternal. No slumber can seize Him nor sleep" (2:225). Verse two of Surah 3 states: "God! There is no god but He—the

Living, the Self-Subsisting, Eternal." In Surah 112, it simply says: "God, the Eternal, Absolute" (v. 2).

Guardian. In Surah 89:14, near the end of the Quran, we read: "For thy Lord is (as a Guardian) on a watchtower." An earlier surah reads: "O mankind! reverence your Guardian-Lord, who created you from a single person, created, of like nature, His mate, and from them twain scattered (like seeds) countless men and women—reverence God, through whom ye demand your mutual (rights), and (reverence) the wombs (that bore you): for God ever watches over you" (4:1).

Holy. "Whatever is in the heavens and on earth, doth declare the Praises and Glory of God—the Sovereign, the Holy One, the Exalted in Might, the Wise" (62:1). God's holiness is also expressed in His goodness, as in 3:26: "In Thy hand is all good." Later, in the same surah, we read: "God loves those who do good" (v. 134).

All-knowing. Surah 35:38 speaks of the scope of God's knowledge. "Verily God knows (all) the hidden things of the heavens and the earth: verily He has full knowledge of all that is in (men's) hearts." An earlier surah also reads: "He knows all that goes into the earth, and all that comes out thereof; all that comes down from the sky and all that ascends thereto."

Lord of all. "And do ye join equals with Him? He is the Lord of (all) the Worlds" (41:9). This theme is also expressed in terms of God's sovereignty, as in these powerful words from Surah 59:23: "God is He, than Whom there is no other god—the Sovereign, the Holy One, the Source of Peace (and Perfection), the Guardian of Faith, the Preserver of Safety, the Exalted in Might, the Irresistible, the Supreme: Glory to God!"

Merciful. "He is the Most Merciful of those who show mercy!" (12:64). The phrase "Oft-forgiving, Most Merciful" is used over and over again in the Quran, six times just in Surah 9 alone. Another powerful expression of God's mercy is given in an earlier surah:

"Those who believed and those who suffered exile and fought (and strove and struggled) in the path of God,—they have the hope of the Mercy of God: And God is Oft-forgiving, Most Merciful."

Revealer. He is the Revealer. The Quran longs for people to trust in God's revelation and expresses astonishment that humans ignore what Allah has shown them. "If only they had stood fast by the Law, the Gospel, and all the revelation that was sent to them from their Lord, they would have enjoyed happiness from every side" (5:56).

In Surah 3 we find a celebration of Jews and Christians who follow Allah's revelation: "And there are, certainly, among the People of the Book, those who believe in God, in the revelation to you, and in the revelation to them, bowing in humility to God: They will not sell the Signs of God for a miserable gain! For them is a reward with their Lord" (v. 199).

Sustainer. One of the more beautiful passages is Surah 7:54, which reads: "Your Guardian Lord is God, Who created the heavens and the earth in six days, and is firmly established on the throne (of authority): He draweth the night as a veil o'er the day, each seeking the other in rapid succession: He created the sun, the moon, and the stars, (all) governed by laws under His command. Is it not His to create and to govern? Blessed be God, the Cherisher and Sustainer of the worlds!"

Worthy Of Worship. This is expressed by stating repeatedly that God is worthy of praise. God himself commands worship, as in 20:14: "Verily, I am God: There is no god but I: So serve thou Me (only), and establish regular prayer for celebrating My praise." Only God can be worshipped. The act of worshiping anyone or anything other than God is a terrible sin, known as shirk. From this, Muslims deny the doctrine of the Trinity and the divinity of Jesus.

Muhammad

The prophet himself is at the center of the Quran, though often as a figure behind every chapter. His name is mentioned only four times, but he is the subject of many passages. Muslims do not believe that Muhammad is writing about himself, however. Islam teaches that Gabriel dictated to Muhammad material that was to be put in the Quran about Muhammad! Further, when the Quran quotes words from Muhammad, Muslims believe that these are words that Allah tells Muhammad to say.

Muhammad has, according to the Quran, an incredible status because Allah called him as a prophet. In fact, he is "the Seal of the Prophets," a phrase from the famous passage in Surah 33 that is used by Muslims to argue that Muhammad is the final prophet. In addition, Muhammad is a judge to his followers (4:65), and is to be respected by them (2:104; 4:46).

Allah himself is a witness to Muhammad's mission (13:43; and 46:8). Further, the Quran teaches that Muhammad's prophetic work was predicted by both Moses (46:10) and by Jesus, of whom the Quran says: "And remember, Jesus, the son of Mary, said: 'O Children of Israel! I am the apostle of God (sent) to you, confirming the Law (which came) before me, and giving Glad Tidings of an Apostle to come after me, whose name shall be Ahmad.'" Ahmad is a shortened form of Muhammad.

Muhammad is the universal messenger from God (34:28), the symbol of Allah's mercy to the world (9:61; 28:46–47; 76:24–26), and inspired by Allah. In Surah 53:10–12 it says: "So did (God) convey the inspiration to His Servant—(conveyed) what He (meant) to convey. The (Prophet's) (mind and) heart in no way falsified that which he saw. Will ye then dispute with him concerning what he saw?"

The Quran describes Muhammad as gentle (3:159), very concerned about his followers (9:128), and in deep distress for unbelievers (12:97; 25:30). It says he was a man of prayer (74:3), and had an "exalted standard of character" (68:4) He was often mocked by his enemies in Mecca, and he was accused of being mad (7:184) and under the power of demons (81:22).

Muhammad is told to adore Allah (96:19), faithfully stick to the message that he is given from God (46:9), follow Allah's duty for him (30:30), and work hard (66:9). In Surah 33, Allah tells Muhammad that he can take women as wives as long as he pays their dowry or if they are "prisoners of war." He can also marry his cousins, and any woman he wants "who dedicates her soul to the Prophet."

Muhammad's followers are told to visit the Prophet's home only when they have permission, to arrive right at mealtime (not before), leave quickly after the meal, and avoid "familiar talk" with the Prophet. It is said that "such (behavior) annoys the Prophet: he is ashamed to dismiss you, but God is not ashamed (to tell you) the truth."

Quran

The Quran also takes up itself as a subject. Satan, we are told, is not the author. Muhammad could not be the author either, since, the Quran argues, he was completely illiterate. Only Allah could have produced such a book. The Quran says of itself that it is clear, understandable, written in pure Arabic, free from error, and that it contains the universal message, one that will guide its hearers into health and into eternal salvation.

Biblical Material

The Quran gives considerable attention to various Old and New Testament figures. According to critics, much of it is derived from Christian and Jewish apocryphal sources. Muslims claim that Islam started with creation and that Allah revealed himself to Jews and

Christians, though both groups altered their scriptures. Muslims use this to explain why Old and New Testament accounts of people and events often differ radically from how they are reported in the Quran.

Of biblical figures, Moses gets the most mention, with more than five hundred verses or almost 10 percent of the text dealing with him. The Quran also gives information about Noah, Abraham, Joshua, David, Jesus, Mary, and others. Muslims find it easy to draw comparisons between Muhammad and Moses the lawgiver, and also with King David, the warrior for God.

Jesus

The Quran treats Jesus with great respect, as a prophet, teacher, and as a Sign from God. It also states that Jesus was born of the Virgin Mary, performed miracles, and that His followers were called Muslims. The Quran also states that it is a serious error to think that Jesus is the Son of God or that God is a trinity of three Persons, as in Christian tradition. For the Quran, Jesus is a prophet, but no more than that.

As said earlier, Muslims do not believe that Jesus died on the Cross. In Surah 4:157, one of the famous verses of the Quran, it speaks about enemies of Allah who insulted the Virgin Mary and who brag: "We killed Christ Jesus the son of Mary, the Apostle of God." The text then reads: "but they killed him not, nor crucified him, but so it was made to appear to them, and those who differ therein are full of doubts, with no (certain) knowledge, but only conjecture to follow, for of a surety they killed him not."

True Believers

Hundreds of verses in the Quran are devoted to a portrait of the true believer. The vast majority of passages deal with behavior, both with the path that is right, and the path that is wrong. This is in keeping with the common assertion that Islam is a religion about the right path, much more than it is a religion about right ideas.

Even though Islam is a religion of law, the Quran is focused more on the larger principles behind the law. These have to do, first of all, with positive things that are expected of all Muslims. The Muslim is a follower of Allah and fears him, and has turned from all false gods. The believer patterns his life after the model of the prophet Muhammad.

The Muslim is a person of prayer and contemplation. He or she is peaceful, faithful, humble, and forgiving. True believers strive to do good works and protect one another. Muslims are to be charitable, according to the Quran, and are to be united in their faith. The disciple of Allah engages in fasting and follows Allah's will on proper marriages and proper inheritance laws. Believers are to remember the rewards of heaven and the pains of hell.

Resistance to evil and sin also identifies the true believer. The Quran teaches that Muslims are to avoid gambling and drinking. Usury is a sin. Certain foods are forbidden, as in Orthodox Judaism. Muslim males cannot have more than four wives. Allah's followers should avoid contact with skeptics and should avoid being too inquisitive about their faith. Sexual lust is wrong, and therefore female believers are to dress modestly.

The Quran warns about the dangers of excess in religion. Muhammad said one time that there were going to be no monks in Islam, referring to a celibate priesthood. This idea of excess also involves avoiding certain ideas. Thus, Surah 4:171 states: "O People of the Book! Commit no excesses in your religion: Nor say of God aught but the truth. Christ Jesus the son of Mary was (no more than) an apostle of God. Say not 'Trinity': desist: it will be better for you: for God is one God: Glory be to Him: (far exalted is He) above having a son."

Unbelievers

The whole human setting of the Quran involves the storm created by Muhammad's prophetic call to decision. His message creates two options: belief or unbelief. There is considerable discussion of those that the Quran calls hypocrites and unbelievers.

Those who reject Allah's message are deaf, blind, and full of disease. They are arrogant, foolish, hate the truth, live in delusion, and their prayers are in vain. The unbeliever is a liar, coward, vain, and a deceiver. Muslims should avoid unbelievers, given their perversity. They will be sent into the depths of hell unless they repent.

Heaven, Hell and Judgment Day

The Quran gives enormous weight to life after death. There are hundreds of verses about paradise, the pains of hell, and the reality of a Final Judgment by God. Though Muslim scholars debate to what extent certain verses about heaven and hell are to be taken literally, the overall message is clear. Heaven is pictured as a garden paradise, with mansions, fountains, food and drink, sexual pleasure, where believers are full of happiness, peace, and joy in the presence of God.

The Quran draws hell as a place of blazing, eternal fire. The unbelievers will taste the boiling fluids of hell, with their faces covered in flame. They will wear garments of fire, will live in eternal regret at the folly of their rebellion against Allah, and will beg for destruction. The Day of Judgment is an absolute certainty, according to the Quran, though the righteous have no reason to fear. Justice will be done and human deeds will be weighed in the balance, when the Last Trumpet sounds.

4

Muslims

The People Called Muslims

Understanding Islam involves coming to grips with the story of Islam through the centuries, the various divisions among Muslims that shape their internal understanding, and a sense of the presence of Islam both globally and in the United States. As well, our appreciation for Islam depends on grasping the major factors that shape the daily life of the Muslim at home, at work, and in society.

Seventy-Five Key Events in Muslim History

In any overview of a world religion, one has to have some sense of the big picture. To that end, we can give brief attention to seventy-five of the most significant events in Muslim history since the death of the prophet Muhammad in AD 632. These dates give one a sense of the breadth of Islamic life and the shape of response in the non-Muslim world to the spread of Islam.

1. 634 Death of Abu Bakr, the first caliph or successor to Muhammad
2. 637 Capture of Jerusalem by Muslim leaders

3. 661 Assassination of Ali, the fourth caliph to Muhammad
4. 680 Murder of Husain, a son of Ali
5. 690 Construction of the Dome of the Rock in Jerusalem
6. 728 Death of Hasan al-Basri, early spiritual leader
7. 732 Muslims defeated at Battle of Tours
8. 750 Rise of the Abbasid Dynasly, based in Baghdad
9. 767 Death of Abu Hanifah, the great legal scholar
10. 925 Death of Abu Bakr al-Razi, one of the great doctors of medicine
11. 950 Death of Al-Farabi, the Muslim Aristotle
12. 1037 Death of Avicenna, a great Islamic philosopher
13. 1099 Crusaders capture Jerusalem
14. 1111 Death of al-Ghazali, second to the Prophet as spiritual leader
15. 1197 Saladin recaptures Jerusalem
16. 1258 Mongols sack Baghdad
17. 1300 Rise of Ottoman Empire
18. 1315 Death of Raymond Lull, Christian missionary to Islam
19. 1453 Ottoman Turks capture Constantinople, and it is renamed Istanbul
20. 1492 End of Muslim Spain
21. 1517 Salim I conquers Egypt
22. 1520 Rise of Sulayman the Magnificent, the Ottoman emperor
23. 1563 Akbar gains power in India
24. 1707 Decline of Muslim power in India
25. 1798 Napoleon in Egypt
26. 1803 Wahhabi movement gains control in Saudi Arabia
27. 1830 France occupies Algeria
28. 1881 British take control of Egypt

29. 1902 Qasim Amin pioneers feminism in Egypt
30. 1910 Oil prospects in Persia
31. 1924 Secularization of Turkey
32. 1928 Muslim Brotherhood founded
33. 1932 Political independence in Iraq
34. 1947 Creation of Pakistan
35. 1948 Founding of the State of Israel
36. 1962 Algeria gains independence
37. 1964 Formation of the Palestinian Liberation Organization
38. 1967 Six Day War between Israel and Egypt
39. 1973 October War between Israel and Arabs
40. 1977 Egyptian President Anwar Sadat makes peace with Israel at Camp David
41. 1979 Islamic revolution in Iran
42. 1979 USSR invades Afghanistan
43. 1981 Assassination of President Sadat
44. 1982 Israeli invasion of Lebanon
45. 1987 Intifada begins in the Occupied Territories of Gaza and the West Bank
46. 1991 Gulf War to liberate Kuwait
47. 1993 Bombing of the World Trade Center
48. 2000 Breakdown of Israeli-Palestinian peace talks
49. 2001 Attack on America (September 11)
50. 2001 U.S. launches military campaign in Afghanistan (October 7)
51. 2002 Terrorist bombing in Bali kills 202 (October 12)
52. 2003 U.S. attacks Iraq (March)
53. 2004 Crisis in Darfur escalates
54. 2004 Madrid train bombings (March 11)
55. 2004 Killing of Dutch filmmaker Theo van Gogh (November 2)

56. 2004 Death of Palestinian Authority President Arafat (November 11)
57. 2005 Mahmoud Abbas elected president of the Palestinian Authority
58. 2005 Rafik Hariri killed in Beirut (February 14)
59. 2005 London bombings (July 7)
60. 2005 Israeli forces leave Gaza and the West Bank (August)
61. 2005 Danish cartoon controversy erupts (September–December)
62. 2006 Hamas defeats Fatah in general election (January)
63. 2006 Arrest of suspected terrorists in Toronto (June 3)
64. 2006 Israeli-Lebanese war (July 12–August 14)
65. 2006 Pope Benedict XVI controversy (September)
66. 2007 Fighting between Hamas and Fatah in Gaza
67. 2007 Muslim and Christian leaders start new dialogue
68. 2008 Gaza under Israeli attack (December 27–January 19, 2009)
69. 2009 U.S. President Barack Obama's Speech in Cairo (June 4)
70. 2010 Negotiations on Israeli-Palestinian conflict
71. 2010 Controversy over mosque proposal at Ground Zero
72. 2010 Florida pastor threatens Quran burning
73. 2011 Egyptian Christians killed after worship service
74. 2011 Referendum on southern Sudan
75. 2011 Revolutions in Tunisia, Egypt, and other Middle East countries

Several themes emerge from an examination of these key events. First, it is obvious that Islam has spread, at least in part, through military might. In fact, the Muslim armies were so powerful that within a hundred years of the Prophet's death, the Islamic empire extended from the edge of China on the east, across the upper part of Africa, to Spain on the west. This is a military conquest almost unmatched in the history of the world.

Second, there is the corresponding reality of the conquest of Muslims by others. The sword has cut both ways. Richard the Lion-Hearted, the famous Crusader, showed little mercy to Muslims, even when they surrendered, even after he promised them safety under his rule. Contemporary Islam has also known military defeat, thanks to empire-building at the hands of the British, French, Germans, and other powers.

Third, the key events also illustrate that Islam has offered a rich intellectual heritage to the world. This has come in terms of art, philosophy, architecture, medicine, jurisprudence, theology, mathematics, and science. In fact, when the Crusaders invaded Muslim lands, under orders to overthrow the barbarians, they were sometimes astonished at the high level of culture of Islam.

Fourth, Muslim leaders have often been politically astute, given the fact that they have had to run empires across vast distances, under diverse social climates, various linguistic realities, and changing military and economic conditions. The staying power of Islamic political life is shown best by the fact that the Muslim Ottoman Empire lasted over six centuries.

There is also a sense, however, that Muslim history illustrates a real decline in power and influence, even before the rise of the Ottoman sultans in the late thirteenth century. To some extent, Muslims continue to struggle with the loss of the "golden age" of Islam and debate among themselves about how to revive those days. A few brave Muslim intellectuals have risked death by calling for focus on internal reasons for Islamic decline rather than blaming Israel and the United States.

Early Muslim Leaders (623–683)

Muhammad (623–32)

First Caliph: Abu Bakr (632–34) father-in-law of prophet

Second Caliph: Umar I (634–44)

Third Caliph: Uthman ibn Affan (644–56) Muhammad's son-in-law and a member of the Umayyad tribe. Uthman was murdered by an Islamic mob.

Fourth Caliph and first Shi'a Imam: Ali Ben Abu Talib (656–61), Muhammad's son-in-law. Ali was resented by Umayyads and was killed in 661.

al-Hasan (661–69), second Imam, grandson of prophet, and older brother of Husayn.

Muawiyah I ibn Abu Sufyan (661–80), first leader of Umayyad dynasty

al-Husayn (669–80) third Imam and grandson of Muhammad. Husayn was killed at Karbala.

Yazid I ibn Muawiyah (680–83), second Umayyad caliph

Traditions in Islam

Like all religions, Islam has not been able to retain its original unity. In fact, within a generation of the Prophet's death, Muslims were at war with each other over political leadership and the proper interpretation of Islamic spirituality. Muslims are usually divided into two main branches although there are many other groups within Islam.

The two biggest branches are: (1) Sunni and (2) Shia, also known as Shiite. Sunni Islam represents the largest grouping in Islam. Of the world's 1.5 billion Muslims, over one billion are Sunni, which is about nine in ten Muslims. Sunni Muslims trace themselves back to the Prophet but separate from Shia Muslims over the question of proper authority in Islam, the shape of Islamic law, and the nature of salvation.

There are approximately 170 million Shia or Shiite Muslims globally. Though they represent a minority among the three main Islamic groups, the Shia version of Islam became the most well known in the West after the Islamic revolution in Iran in 1979. The Shah of Iran was deposed and the Ayatollah Khomeini, the well-known Muslim leader, returned from exile in France to run the country.

In Sunni Islam, the imam is the person who leads prayer in the mosque. The same word in Shia Islam stands both for leaders like the Ayatollah but, most importantly, for the succession of singular figures said to be chosen by Allah to guide Islam in its earliest and most important years. One Shia group believes there were seven imams, while another extends the number to twelve. In each group the last imam is believed to be alive, but he has been placed in a state of hiddenness by Allah.

Shia Muslims give enormous significance to the martyrdom of Husein, whose father Ali, was the son-in-law of the Prophet. Husein and fellow Muslims were slaughtered by Sunni Muslims at Kerbala in Iraq on the tenth day of the Muslim month of Muharran in AD 680. Every year Shia Muslims engage in eleborate rituals to honor Husein's memory. Shia pilgrims travel to his shrine in Kerbala every year.

There is a third tradition in Islam that is mystical. This tradition is Sufi. Both Sunni and Shia Muslims can be Sufi. Accoding to some estimates, they number more than 240 million throughout the world. Sufism emerged when Islam became decadent, materialistic, and lazy in the twilight years of the earliest Muslim dynasties. Al-Ghazzali, the great Islamic devotional writer, turned to Sufism as an alternative to the speculative, uncertain paths of philosophy and reason. The Sufi path is best known through the "whirling dervish," a type of dance used to resist outside stimuli and focus on the mind of Allah.

Sufi Orders

Order	Founder	Dominant influence
Naqshbandiyyah	Baha al Din Naqshband (d. 1389) from Bukhara	North Africa to China, Europe, and America
Qadiriyyah	Abd al Qadir al Jilani (1077–1166) from Iraq	Central Asia to South Africa, Morocco to Malaysia
Tijaniyyah	Ahmad al Tijani (d. 1815) from Algeria	Sub-Saharan Africa
Shadiliyyah	Abul-Hassan al Shadili (d. 1258) from Morocco	Egypt and North Africa
Rifa'iyyah	Ahmad ibn Ali al Rifai (d. 1182) from southern Iraq	Muslim world
Suhrawardiyyah	Abu Najib Suhrawardi (d. 1168) from Persia	India
Kubrawiyyah	Najm al Din Kubra (d. 1221) from Khawarzm	Central Asia
Mawlawiyyah	Jalal al Din Rumi (d. 1273) from Persia	Turkey
Chishtiyyah	Muin al Din Chishti (d. 1236) from Persia	India
Khalwatiyyah	Umar al Khalwati (d. 1397) from Persia	Syria , Lebanon, North Africa, and Balkans
Yashrutiyyah	Ali Nur al Din al Yashruti (d.1892) from Palestine	Syria and Lebanon
Badawiyyah	Ahmad al Badawi (d. 1276) from Morocco	Egypt and Sudan

There are also several groups that are viewed as heretical by most Muslims. The most famous of these sects are: (1) the Bahai, (2) the Ahmadis, and (3) the Druze. Bahais and the Ahmadis have been subject to terrible persecution, even martyrdom. The Druze number about a million followers and are primarily located in Lebanon, Syria, and Palestine.

Bahais focus on their leader Baha'u'llah (1817–92) as the final prophet for mankind, while the Druze believe the same of al-Hakim, an Egyptian of the eleventh century.

The Ahmadi movement was founded by Mirza Ghulam Ahmad Qadiyani (d. 1908), who also was proclaimed as the ultimate prophet, a notion contrary to the prevailing Muslim view that Muhammad is the "seal" of the prophets.

Muslims in the Global Context

One in every six persons on the planet is a Muslim. Islam is the second largest religion, with well over 1 billion followers. There are Muslims in all the distinct nations of the world. Islam is truly a global religion, even though it is often dismissed as an Arab religion, a view countered by the fact that there are more non-Arab Muslims in Indonesia than there are Arab Muslims in any individual Arab nation.

From the beginning, Muslims have viewed the world in two parts: those areas under the control of Islam and those outside. In terms of the current global situation, the CIA Factbook lists 237 nations. Of these, Islam is the majority religion in 55 different countries, and a significant minority religion in another 26 nations. This means that Islam has a powerful presence in almost one third of the countries in the world.

The countries where Islam is in the majority are: Afghanistan, Albania, Algeria, Azerbaijan, Bahrain, Bangladesh, Bosnia and

Herzegovina, Brunei, Burkina Faso, Chad, Cocos (Keeling) Islands, Comoros, Cote d'Ivoire, Djibouti, Egypt, Eritrea, Gambia, Gaza Strip, Guinea, Guinea-Bissau, Indonesia, Iran, Iraq, Jordan, Kazakhstan, Kosovo, Kuwait, Kyrgyzstan, Lebanon, Libya, Maldives, Mali, Mauritania, Mayotte, Morocco, Niger, Nigeria, Oman, Pakistan, Qatar, Saudi Arabia, Senegal, Sierra Leone, Somalia, Sudan, Syria, Tajikistan, Tunisia, Turkey, Turkmenistan, United Arab Emirates, Uzbekistan, West Bank, Western Sahara, and Yemen.

Muslims represent a significant minority in many other nations including: Benin, Cyprus, Ethiopia, Georgia, Ghana, India, Israel, Liberia, Macedonia, Malawi, Malaysia, Mauritius, Mozambique, Singapore, Suriname, Swaziland, Tanzania, Uganda, Yugoslavia, and Zambia.

The term minority can be misleading, since there are over 100 million Muslims in India. While the Middle East constitutes the heartland of Islam, the largest number of Muslims are found in Bangladesh, India, Indonesia, and Pakistan. In fact, more than 40 percent of the entire Muslim population of the world is located in these four countries.

Islam in the United States

There are about 3 million Muslims in America, and there are estimates that within fifteen years Islam will bypass Judaism as the second largest religious grouping in America, next to Christianity. Muslims first came to America as slaves from Africa in the late 1700s. Muslim immigration began in the late nineteenth century, continuing in two surges just before and after World War I, after World War II, and again when President Johnson relaxed immigration laws in 1967.

Islam first came to public attention in America when Alexander Russell Webb, a Muslim convert, defended Islam at the first Parliament of the World's Religions held in Chicago in 1893. Webb helped build the first mosque in the USA. When Muslims immigrated to the American Midwest in the early 1900s, mosques were built first in Ross, North Dakota, and then one in Highland Park, Michigan, in 1919.

The various branches of Islam are all represented in America. Sunni Muslims dominate, as in the rest of the Muslim world. There are a number of Shia mosques and centers throughout America, including a branch of the Ismaeli group that follows Prince Aga Khan. There are also over forty separate Sufi groups active in the country, including the Sufi Order brought to America in 1910 by its founder, Pir Hazrat Inayat Khan.

The rise of the Black Muslim movement represents a fascinating aspect of Islam in the United States. Its roots lie in a resurgence of Black nationalism at the turn of the twentieth century, symbolized most significantly in the work of Marcus Garvey (1887–1940), a central figure in the Rastafarian movement, and Noble Drew Ali (1886–1929) founder of the Moorish Science Temple, another Black nationalist group.

Black nationalism took its formative shape through the influence of Fard Muhammad, who started preaching the Black Muslim message in Detroit in July 1930, and founded the Nation of Islam (NOI). Although he disappeared after four years, he influenced a man named Elijah Muhammad who heard Fard in 1930. Elijah Muhammad, born in 1897, accepted Fard's message about the supremacy of the Black race and the devilish nature of the white race.

Elijah Muhammad moved to Chicago in 1932 and led the NOI movement until his death in 1975. He was a controversial leader, not only because of his racist views, but also due to his extramarital affairs that shocked his Nation of Islam, including Malcolm X, one of Elijah Muhammad's most famous followers. Malcolm X, born as Malcolm Little in 1925, converted to Islam in 1948, joined the NOI in 1953, and became a leader in the movement.

50 Most Influential Muslims

1. His Majesty King Abdullah bin Abdul Aziz Al Saud, King of Saudi Arabia, Custodian of the Two Holy Mosques

2. His Eminence Grand Ayatollah Hajj Sayyid Ali Khamenei, Supreme Leader of the Islamic Republic of Iran

3. His Majesty King Mohammed VI, King of Morocco

4. His Majesty King Abdullah II bin Al Hussein, King of the Hashemite Kingdom of Jordan

5. His Excellency Recep Tayyip Erdogan, Prime Minister of the Republic of Turkey

6. His Majesty Sultan Qaboos bin Sa'id al Sa'id, Sultan of Oman

7. His Eminence Grand Ayatollah Sayyid Ali Hussein Sistani, Marja of the Hawza, Najaf

8. His Eminence Sheikh Al Azhar Dr. Muhammad Sayyid Tantawi, Grand Sheikh of the Al Azhar University, Grand Imam of Al Azhar Mosque

9. Sheikh Dr. Yusuf Qaradawi, Head of the International Union of Muslim Scholars

10. His Eminence Sheikh Dr. Ali Goma'a, Grand Mufti of the Arab Republic of Egypt

11. His Eminence Sheikh Abdul Aziz Ibn Abdullah Aal al Sheikh, Grand Mufti of the Kingdom of Saudi Arabia

12. Mohammad Mahdi Akef, Supreme Guide of the Muslim Brotherhood

13. Hodjaefendi Fethullah Gullen, Turkish Muslim Preacher

14. Amr Khaled, Preacher and Social Activist

15. Hajji Mohammed Abd al Wahhab, Ameer of the Tablighi Jamaat, Pakistan

16. His Royal Eminence Amirul Mu'minin Sheikh as Sultan Muhammadu Sa'adu Abubakar III, Sultan of Sokoto

17. Seyyed Hasan Nasrallah, Secretary General of Hezbollah

18. Dr. KH Achmad Hasyim Muzadi, Chairman of Nahdlatul Ulama, Indonesia

19. Sheikh Salman al Ouda, Saudi Scholar and Educator

20. His Highness Shah Karim al Hussayni, The Aga Khan IV, 49th Imam of the Ismaili Muslims

21. His Highness Emir Sheikh Mohammed bin Rashid al Maktoum, Ruler of Dubai, Prime Minister of the United Arab Emirates

22. His Highness General Sheikh Mohammed bin Zayed al Nahyan, Crown Prince of Abu Dhabi and Deputy Supreme Commander of the United Arab Emirates Armed Forces

23. Sheikh Dr. M Sa'id Ramadan al Bouti, Leading Islamic Scholar in Syria

24. His Majesty Sultan Haji Hassanal Bolkiah Mu'izzaddin Waddaulah, Sultan and Yang Di-Pertuan of Brunei Darussalam

25. His Eminence Professor Dr. Sheikh Ahmad Muhammad al Tayeb, President of Al Azhar University

26. His Eminence Mohammad bin Mohammad al Mansour, Imam of the Zaidi Sect of Shi'a Muslims

27. His Eminence Justice Sheikh Muhammad Taqi Usmani, Leading Scholar of Islamic Jurisprudence, Pakistan

28. His Excellency President Abdullah Gul, President of the Republic of Turkey

29. Sheikh Mohammad Ali al Sabouni, Scholar of *Tafsir*

30. His Eminence Sheikh Abdullah Bin Bayyah, Deputy-Head of the International Union of Muslim Scholars

31. Her Eminence Sheikha Munira Qubeysi, Leader of the Qubeysi Movement

32. His Eminence Sheikh Ahmad Tijani Ali Cisse, Leader of Tijaniyya Sufi Order

33. Sheikh al Habib Umar bin Hafiz, Director of Dar al Mustafa, Tarim, Yemen

34. Khaled Mashaal, Leader of Hamas

35. Professor Dr. M. Din Syamsuddin, Chairman of Muhammadiyya, Indonesia

36. Maulana Mahmood Madani, Secretary General of Jamiat Ulemae-Hind, India

37. Sheikh Habib Ali Zain al Abideen al Jifri, Director General of the Tabah Foundation, United Arab Emirates

38. Sheikh Hamza Yusuf Hanson, Founder of Zaytuna Institute, USA

39. His Eminence Sheikh Professor Dr. Mustafa Ceric, Grand Mufti of Bosnia and Herzegovina

40. His Excellency Professor Dr. Ekmelledin Ihsanoglu, Secretary General of the Organization of the Islamic Conference

41. General Mohammad Ali Jafari, Commander of the Revolutionary Guard, Iran

42. Dato' Haji Nik Abdul Aziz Nik Mat, Religious Guide of the Islamic Party of Malaysia

43. Motiur Rahman Nizami, Ameer of the Jamaat-e-Islami, Bangladesh

44. Professor Sayid Ameen Mian Qaudri, Barelwi Leader and Spiritual Guide

45. His Holiness Dr. Syedna Mohammad Burhannuddin Saheb, 52nd Da'i l-Mutlaq of the Dawoodi Bohras

46. Dr. Abdul Qadeer Khan, Pakistani Nuclear Scientist

47. Professor Dr. Seyyed Hossein Nasr, Islamic Philosopher

48. Abdullah 'Aa Gym' Gymnastiar, Indonesian Preacher

49. Sheikh Mehmet Nazim Adil al Qubrusi al Haqqani, Leader of Naqshbandi-Haqqani Sufi Order

50. His Excellency Dr. Abd al Aziz bin Uthman Altwaijiri, Secretary General of the Islamic Educational, Scientific and Cultural

This list is from John Esposito and Ibrahim Kalin, eds. *The 500 Most Influential Muslims in the World* (Royal Islamic Strategic Studies Centre, 2009).

In April 1963, Malcolm X confronted Elijah about his adultery and the leader simply tried to rationalize his behavior. That led to some estrangement between the two, heightened by comments Malcolm X made about President Kennedy's assassination in November. Malcolm X left the Nation of Islam in early 1964, and was killed by three of its radical members on February 21, 1965.

The role of Malcolm X was then picked up by Louis Farrakhan (b. May 11, 1933) who became Elijah's National Minister in 1965 and minister of the movement's famous mosque in Harlem. After Elijah's death ten years later, Farrakhan had increasing disagreements with Wallace Deen Muhammad, Elijah's son and successor. From 1975 through 1985, Wallace steered the Nation of Islam on a more moderate course, shut it down in 1985, and emerged as a major Sunni leader in the United States.

These changes did not sit well with Farrakhan, who declared in November of 1977 that he was re-creating the Nation of Islam on the more radical teachings of Elijah Muhammad. In the last quarter of a century Farrakhan has become one of the most powerful and controversial Black leaders in America. On October 6, 1995, he led the Million Man March for Blacks in Washington. That same year, his infamy grew as he offered O. J. Simpson's attorneys the protection of the Nation of Islam. There was also news of a plot to kill him by the daughter of Malcolm X, who believed that Farrakhan was behind the assassination of her father.

The Shape of a Muslim Life

This chapter gives some sense of the breadth of Islamic history, the various divisions within Islam, and some of the significant aspects of the Muslim story in the United States. Apart from all of this complexity, what can be said about the common patterns in the Muslim's personal, social, economic, and moral life? Obviously, no two Muslims are alike. In spite of this, what can be generally expected as one becomes friends with a devout Muslim on the streets of Washington or Cairo or in Jammu in northern India?

Beyond the rhythms of Islamic religious life, we can expect most Muslims to be hospitable, especially in the Arab world. Most devout Muslims will obey the dietary laws of Islam, so we will not be served alcohol or pork. When spending time with our Muslim friends, we will not be invited to gamble. If we are invited to a Muslim's home, we should avoid making comment on the person's possessions, since that could be taken as an indication that you want these for your home.

Many Muslims would have moral objections to abortion, suicide, and homosexuality, though Arab males are very demonstrative in their friendships. Muslims have some openness to birth control. We might notice some charms and amulets in a Muslim home, though these are generally frowned upon by the tradition. It would be very rude to show the bottom of your feet to any Muslim or greet him with the left hand.

There is a very relaxed attitude towards time in much of the Islamic world, especially in the Middle East and Africa, so if you are planning something with a Muslim from those regions understand that the person might be late. The phrase "if Allah wills" might accompany any suggestions about time commitments. This phrase is also often used in reference to hopes and future aspirations. Muslims from various countries might be tough in bartering, but Islam demands honesty once agreements are made. No interest is to be charged on any business transactions.

A devout Muslim will expect you to respect their faith and may not be open to debate. It is likely that most Muslims you might befriend will not understand why the West is unsympathetic toward Islam, believes that Islam has no respect for human rights, and does not respect women. Most devout Muslims will also be committed to spreading Islam to the whole world, as the Prophet commanded.

Most Muslims regard themselves in unity with the whole Islamic community, even as they express disagreements with those branches of Islam not their own. They will harbor a sense of anger over Western mistreatment of Muslims, particularly in the case of the Palestinians. You may see overt anti-Semitism, particularly in myths about a global Jewish conspiracy.

Most Muslim will not tolerate any attacks on the credibility of the Prophet or the Quran. For a devout believer, these are fundamentals not up for debate. That person may not understand why you cannot see the beauty of the Prophet and the miracle of the Quran. The person will have as difficult a time understanding why Christians believe in a Trinity and that Jesus died on a cross as Christians have understanding why Muslims believe in the Prophet and the Quran. A Muslim will really believe that the message of the Quran is Allah's word to the whole world in a similar way to how Christians view the Bible.

Countries and Freedom

Muslim Country	% Muslim	Political Rights	Civil Rights	Freedom Rating
Afghanistan	99%	6	6	NF
Albania	70%	3	3	PF
Algeria	99%	6	5	NF
Azerbaijan	93.4%	6	5	NF
Bahrain	81.2%	6	5	PF
Bangladesh	89.5%	3	4	PF
Bosnia-Herzegovina	40%	4	3	PF
Brunei	67%	6	5	NF
Burkina Faso	50%	5	3	F
Chad	53.1%	7	6	NF
Comoros	98%	3	4	PF
Cote d'Ivoire	38.6%	6	5	NF
Djibouti	94%	5	5	PF
Egypt	90%	6	5	NF
Gambia	90%	5	5	PF
Guinea	85%	7	6	NF
Guinea-Bissau	50%	4	4	PF
Indonesia	86.1%	2	3	F
Iran	98%	6	6	NF
Iraq	97%	5	6	NF
Jordan	92%	6	5	NF
Kazakhstan	47%	6	5	NF
Kosovo	90%	5	4	PF
Kuwait	85%	4	4	PF
Kyrgyzstan	75%	6	5	NF

Muslim Country	% Muslim	Political Rights	Civil Rights	Freedom Rating
Lebanon	59.7%	5	3	PF
Libya	97%	7	7	NF
Malaysia	60%	4	4	PF
Maldives	60.4%	3	4	PF
Mali	90%	2	3	F
Mauritania	100%	6	5	NF
Morocco	98.7%	5	4	PF
Niger	80%	5	4	PF
Nigeria	50%	5	4	PF
Oman	75%	6	5	NF
Pakistan	95%	4	5	PF
Qatar	77.5%	6	5	NF
Saudi Arabia	100%	7	6	NF
Senegal	94%	3	3	PF
Sierra Leone	60%	3	3	F
Somalia	100%	7	7	NF
Sudan	70%	7	7	NF
Syria	74%	7	6	NF
Tajikistan	90%	6	5	NF
Tunisia	98%	7	5	NF
Turkey	99.8%	3	3	PF
Turkmenistan	89%	7	7	NF
United Arab Emirates	96%	6	5	NF
Uzbekistan	88%	7	7	NF
Yemen	99%	6	5	NF

The ratings on rights and freedom are those of Freedom House. On a scale of 1–7, the lower the number the better the rating for political and civil rights. NF=Not Free PF=Partly Free F=Free

5

Women

Women in Islam

The immense volume of literature on the subject of women in Islam reveals a dramatic division of opinion. The difference is so extreme that one wonders if the same subject is being debated.

On the one hand, orthodox Muslims believe that women gain true freedom in Islam, that the Prophet liberated females, that there is essential equality between males and females, and that non-Muslims have misunderstood the whole topic. On the opposite extreme, critics of Islam argue that women are in bondage in Islam, that the Prophet was a chauvinist, and that the Quran contains very offensive material about women. Many non-Muslims believe that Islamic law and tradition treat women as second-class citizens, and that women are subject to abuse in most Muslim countries of the world.

Orthodox Islamic Ideals

In understanding the place of women in Islam, we can start with a listing of very positive ideals that are taught in orthodox Islam. These principles may not always be followed, but they present the orthodox Islamic teaching in its best light. Here are fifteen key points gathered from various Muslim authors, including Hammudah Abdalati and Jamal A. Badawi, two respected Muslim authorities.

1. The Quran teaches against the view that women are inferior to men.
2. Islam stopped the practice of female infanticide in the Arab world.
3. Women are equal to men but have different roles.
4. Women are allowed to receive education just like men.
5. Women are to be given freedom of expression.
6. Marriage and family life are very sacred.
7. Motherhood is given incredible honor in Islam.
8. Husbands are to love their wives and treat them kindly.
9. Husbands are to make sure their wives are satisfied sexually.
10. The separation of females in worship is done for reasons of purity.
11. Divorce is to be allowed only when absolutely necessary.
12. Women receive a just inheritance in Islamic family law.
13. Veiling of Muslim women is done for protection and purity.
14. The seclusion of women is practiced for reasons of social purity.
15. Polygamy is allowed only if all wives can be supported and loved.

In one of Badawi's essays on the status of women he quotes Surah 4:1 from the Quran: "O mankind! reverence your Guardian-Lord, who created you from a single person, created, of like nature, His mate, and from them twain scattered (like seeds) countless men and women."

Of this passage, Badawi writes:

> In the midst of the darkness that engulfed the world, the divine
> revelation echoed in the wide desert of Arabia with a fresh, noble,
> and universal message to humanity." He then cites an unnamed
> scholar on the same text: "It is believed that there is no text, old or
> new, that deals with the humanity of the woman from all aspects
> with such amazing brevity, eloquence, depth, and originality as
> this divine decree.

Despite this glowing rhetoric, the debate about women in Islam
is not settled so quickly or simply. Difficult questions remain about
the above points, and other concerns are raised as well, including
criticisms of the way the Prophet treated women. Are women really
viewed as equal in the Quran? Is veiling and seclusion truly helpful
to women? Is polygamy compatible with the freedom of women?

The Quran on Women

Some of the lofty principles noted above find solid support in
the Quran. The Quran affirms the unity of males and females in
the original creation by Allah. There are at least fifteen passages
in the Quran that make this point, including Surah 7:189, which
reads: "It is He Who created you from a single person, and made his
mate of like nature, in order that he might dwell with her (in love)."

Further, the Quran teaches that women will be rewarded for
their labor by Allah, just like men:

> For Muslim men and women—for believing men and women, for
> devout men and women, for true men and women, for men and
> women who are patient and constant, for men and women who
> humble themselves, for men and women who give in charity, for
> men and women who fast (and deny themselves), for men and
> women who guard their chastity, and for men and women who

engage much in God's praise—for them has God prepared forgiveness and great reward (33:35).

The Quran also describes husbands and wives as friends (4:36),
and says that there is to be "tranquility, love and mercy" between
them (30:21). In heaven, there will be delight, love, and joy between
spouses (36:55–57, 55:51–53). If divorce occurs in this life, women
are to be treated with grace (2:237) and justice (2:231; 65:2), and
there should be arbitration in conflict (4:35).

Critics of Islam point to other passages, however, to complain
about the status and treatment of women in the Quran. The
dominant charges are: (1) the Quran teaches that the testimony
of women is worth only half that of males; (2) the Quran grants
more power to husbands in the divorce process than is given to
wives; (3) the Quran often grants greater inheritance rights to males
than females; (4) the Quran grants men access to female slaves
for sexual purposes; (5) the Quran allows polygamy for males;
and (6) the Quran actually teaches that husbands are superior to
wives and can beat them.

Muslim apologists admit to the factual reality of these points
but seek to blunt criticism by arguing that (1) the Quranic teaching
improved the status of women in contrast to pre-Islamic Arabic
life, (2) social conditions explain the need for polygamy, or for
the differences about legal testimony and inheritance rights, (3)
military realities of Muhammad's day warrant the use of female
slaves, and (4) Allah's Word is to be trusted and not treated with
suspicion and doubt.

The idea that a husband can beat his wife is rooted in Surah 4:34,
which reads: "Men are the protectors and maintainers of women,
because God has given the one more (strength) than the other, and
because they support them from their means." The verse continues:
"As to those women on whose part ye fear disloyalty and ill-conduct,

admonish them (first), (Next), refuse to share their beds, (And last) beat them (lightly)."

Many ancient and modern Muslim authorities have accepted the plain meaning of the text. For example, Abdullatif Mushtahiri, a contemporary scholar, writes:

> If admonishing and sexual desertion fail to bring forth results and the woman is of a cold and stubborn type, the Quran bestows on man the right to straighten her out by way of punishment and beating, provided he does not break her bones nor shed blood. Many a wife belongs to this querulous type and requires this sort of punishment to bring her to her senses! (*You Ask and Islam Answers*, p. 94)

Muhammad and Women

The teaching of the Prophet on women and the example he set with women is crucial in understanding the Islamic heritage about women. Obviously, Muhammad would affirm all of the ideal principles noted earlier. Muslims love to cite stories from the hadith about his care for girls, his concern about women who were being mistreated, and about his tender relations with Khadijah, his first wife.

Critics of Islam target Muhammad for some of the same things noted in the Quranic material. Thus, Muhammad is viewed as a male chauvinist because of his views on inheritance rights, legal value of a woman's testimony, male dominance in divorce proceedings, and the inferiority of women. Critics also question Muhammad's moral character in terms of his engagement in polygamy, sexual use of female slaves, and defense of the Quran when it teaches that wives can be beaten.

Muslim apologists use the same arguments to defend the Prophet as they do for defending the Quran. However, they also have to address other things that surfaced in the course of Muhammad's life.

These include complaints that the Prophet: (1) taught that there are more women in hell than men, (2) believed brief contractual marriages are sometimes right, given the sexual needs of males, (3) married one of his wives when she was just six years old, (4) married his own stepson's wife, (5) taught that women are mentally inferior to men, and (6) believed that the prayer of a man is invalid if a donkey, dog, or woman walks in front of him while praying.

Contrary to what non-Muslims might think, these allegations were not invented by enemies of Muhammad. Islamic scholars grant that each point arises out of genuine hadith about the Prophet. In other words, there is no dispute over the basic facts. The differences come over how to interpret them, whether a person accepts or rejects the Prophet's teaching, and whether his behavior is justified or condemned.

For the orthodox Muslim, it is absolutely unthinkable that the Prophet can be wrong in his views or in his deeds. So, if the Prophet taught, for example, that women outnumber men in hell, then that is a truth that is to be accepted. If he taught that women are mentally inferior, that is the case. If he advocated brief contractual marriages, then he was right to do so. Who is anyone to question the word of the Prophet, at least according to the orthodox Muslim view of the prophet?

The story of Muhammad's marriage to Aisha when she was six illustrates how one's fundamental worldview determines perspective and judgment. According to the hadith, Muhammad did in fact marry her when she was six, though he did not consummate his marriage until she was nine.

Muslim scholars have gone to great lengths to defend the Prophet. Some argue that Aisha was much older, in her mid-teens, when the Prophet first slept with her. Another author states that by marrying Aisha so early, she was given a longer time to know the great Prophet.

Other Muslims simply declare that Allah gave Aisha to the Prophet at age six in marriage, and that there is absolutely nothing wrong with him sleeping with her at age nine. This was the will of Allah, the perfect Creator, for his sinless Prophet. One writer states: "Only in Islam can one with good conscience accept 'the whole package' without ignorantly or hypocritically denying things that they don't like. This is how true internal

> ### Irshad Manji
>
> Irshad Manji (b. 1968) is one of the most influential Muslim feminists in the world. Author of *The Trouble with Islam Today*, Manji is a Canadian public intellectual who is pro-lesbian, pro-democratic, pro-Palestinian, and pro-Israeli. *The New York Times* called her "Osama bin Laden's worst nightmare." She is Director of the Moral Courage Project at New York University and the creator of the PBS documentary *Faith without Fear*.
>
> www.irshadmanji.com

peace and balance are achieved." (Robert Squires, "The Young Marriage of Aisha," at www.islamic-awareness.org)

The Issue of Female Circumcision

In recent years the world community has been alarmed by the practice of female circumcision, which is also known as Female Genital Mutilation (FGM). This ritual is done in approximately thirty countries worldwide. It involves several medical procedures, which include removal of some or all of the female genitalia. The World Health Organization reports that nearly three million girls go through this rite every year.

Muslim leaders throughout history have defended female circumcision on the basis of various alleged sayings of Muhammad. Even in recent years these sayings of Muhammad, and some material in the Quran, have been used to defend both male and female circumcision. About a decade ago, some Egyptian clerics wanted to have a fatwa (ruling) that called for the death penalty for a Muslim judge who did not favor male circumcision. An Egyptian court

Militant Islamic Laws Regarding Women: The Taliban

Cannot receive education

Cannot be employed

Must remain at home unless absolutely necessary

Cannot be doctors

Cannot associate with any male who is not a relative

Cannot wear nail polish or any makeup

Cannot have hair cut

Must wear the veil (*burqa*) at all times outside the home

Violation of dress code will result in public lashings

Breaking of sexual rules will result in stoning

Transported by special buses with windows covered

ruled that female circumcision could not be outlawed because of certain sayings of the Prophet that seemed to favor it.

Some Muslim leaders seek to defend female circumcision by arguing that it protects young girls from sexual temptation. One writer argued that the experience of going through the rite is actually beneficial in other ways too, since the young girl receives presents, and she is surrounded by a loving community, and the incredible support gives her a better sense of self. Other Muslim leaders challenge the view that Islam mandates female circumcision.

Women in Modern Islam

As complex as the debate is over the ideals of Islamic orthodoxy, it is obviously much more difficult to write with accuracy about the actual realities of life for Muslim women in a global perspective.

Given the number of Muslim women in the world, the diversity of Muslim states, the power of feminism, the only thing that can be written with certainty is that no one picture can capture what it is like to be a Muslim woman in our day.

Here are some snapshots that capture the diverse realities gathered from books, newspaper reports, and Web sites.

- In Britain and other Western countries, secular women are turning to Islam as an alternative to a materialistic culture that treats women as objects for sexual gratification.

- In Jordan, rape victims find themselves cut off from their families and even killed because of the shame brought to the home because of the loss of virginity. Honor killings are illegal, and both the king and queen speak against the practice.

- Sister Power! operates a Web site to bring skilled Muslim women together to increase job opportunities and increase business success.

Asma Gull Hasan

Asma Gull Hasan calls herself "the Muslim feminist cowgirl." She was born in Chicago but was raised in Colorado. Hasan plays a prominent role in shaping public opinion about Islam. She is author of *Why I Am a Muslim* and *American Muslims: The New Generation*. She is also an editor of *The American Muslim* and a contributor to the website www.isufirock.com.

Hasan combines her love for the United States with a love for her Islamic faith, but much of traditional Islam may not be open to her. In her book *American Muslims: The Next Generation* she states: "I'm tired of Muslim women having to make concessions, like sitting somewhere else besides the position of honor (which is in the front of the mosque) or wearing *hijab* (a special head covering for women) because men can't control themselves."

Hasan is a powerful example of a free-spirited Muslim woman. She is willing to confront traditional Islam but says that she does so because of her deep trust in Allah and Muhammad.

www.asmahasan.com

- In Saudi Arabia, princesses obey Muslim law while in Saudi Arabia, but behave differently when visiting Western countries.

- In one Middle East country, a woman had acid thrown in her face because she allowed a wisp of hair to appear from beneath her head covering.

- Fareena Alam, a Bengali woman living in London, started the Web site "Islam—The Modern Religion" at age eighteen. She believes that "Islam's attitude toward women is a dream come true for anyone who is interested in equal rights and feminism."

- A Canadian woman converted to Islam from a liberal Protestant church. She lost her two children in a custody suit with her non-Muslim ex-husband. At her mother's funeral, she was told by her uncle, a Christian pastor: "When we bury her, we bury you."

- Karamah, an organization of Muslim female lawyers, monitors human rights abuses from its base in Fairfax, Virginia. They protest abuses of women by Muslim leaders around the world.

- A Muslim woman from the Middle East became a Christian and was tortured for her decision. Her face now shows marks of the brutality. She fled to Canada to escape threats of death.

- In January 2000 the Taliban relaxed some of their rules about girls being educated, allowing the establishment of private schools that were open to females.

The diversity among Muslim women is obvious. Views that all Muslim women are enslaved or imprisoned are incorrect. In 2002 one of the most powerful Muslims in Lebanon was a woman.

Of course, in spite of such cases, there are countries and situations where Muslim women have little freedom. *The Globe* and *Mail* (Toronto) did a report in 2009 on women in Kandahar, Afghanistan. Their stories about child brides and physical assaults on young women make depressing reading.

6

Jihad, Terrorism, and September 11

September 11, 2001, has forever altered the significance of the word jihad to the modern world. While many Muslims assert that the word simply means spiritual struggle, militant Islam has a far more sinister understanding: "Holy War."

In February 1998, three and a half years before September 11, Osama bin Laden made his own views clear. Along with other extremists from Egypt, Pakistan, and Bangladesh, he issued a fatwa or ruling that called on Muslims "to kill the Americans and their allies—civilian and military." He said that this is "an individual duty for every Muslim who can do it in any country in which it is possible to do it" (See Kepel and Milelli, *Al Qaeda in its Own Words*, p. 55). In the winter of 2001, Osama bin Laden implied in an interview with ABC News producer Rahimullah Yousafsai that he would kill his own children, if necessary, in order to hit American targets.

In contrast, the vast majority of Muslim states have opposed Osama bin Laden since September 11. Here is one news report of enormous significance for world peace: "Iran has vehemently condemned the suicidal terrorist attacks in the United States and has expressed its deep sorrow and sympathy with the American nation"

(Iran Today, September 24, front page report). The governments of Bahrain, Egypt, Lebanon, Oman, Pakistan, Palestine, Qatar, Saudi Arabia, Turkey, United Arab Emirates, and Yemen also expressed their condemnation of the terrorist attacks.

American Muslim groups condemned the terrorist attack immediately. One prominent group issued this press release on September 12:

> The Islamic Supreme Council of America (ISCA) categorically condemns yesterday's airline hijackings and attacks against the World Trade Center, the Pentagon, and all other targets. From coast to coast, we join our neighbors, co-workers and friends across ethnic, cultural and religious lines in mourning the devastating loss of precious life, which Islam holds as sacred. We pray for the thousands of innocent victims, for their families, for law enforcement and emergency workers, for stranded travelers, and for all whose confidence and security have been shaken. We pray that God's Infinite Mercy reaches us all.

The tragedies of September 11 have brought to the surface a long and bitter struggle between Muslims over the meaning of jihad and the nature of true Islam. These contemporary conflicts about Islam's real identity lie in ancient debates about the teaching of the Quran, the example of the Prophet, the legitimacy of non-Muslim governments, and the place of war in Islamic ideology.

Background to the Two Islams

The current debates between Muslims about jihad are better understood when the following crucial facts are noted. Anyone who reads even briefly on the history and nature of Islam will discover these items to be beyond dispute, though what these facts mean is a source of considerable debate.

Jihad, Terrorism, and September 11 65

- The Quran uses the term *jihad* to mean personal spiritual struggle.

- The Quran also uses *jihad* in reference to "holy war" or just war.

- The Prophet engaged in battles of war.

- The Prophet taught that Islam must be spread to the whole world.

- Islamic law justifies self-defense and certain acts of war.

- Muslims conquered non-Arab lands and peoples through war.

- Muslims divide the world into two: Islam and non-Islam.

- Many Muslims believe that all countries should follow Islamic law.

- Many Muslim countries are authoritarian rather than democratic and do not tolerate dissent.

Out of the mix of these realities essentially two different perspectives among Muslims have emerged. The vast majority of Muslims believe that none of the above points justify terrorism. They believe that the Quranic defense of war does not apply to the attacks of September 11. They believe that Osama bin Laden would be condemned by the Prophet, that he has broken Islamic law, that he has disgraced Islam, and is doomed to eternal punishment.

Muslim extremists believe the opposite. They view their actions as a true jihad or "holy war" against infidels and the enemies of Islam. They believe it is right to target America, "the great Satan." Osama bin Laden believes that the Quran supports his campaign, that the Prophet would bless his cause, that Islamic law justifies

Negative View of al-Qaeda

More than nine-in-ten (94%) Muslims in Lebanon express negative opinions of al-Qaeda, as do majorities of Muslims in Turkey (74%), Egypt (72%), Jordan (62%) and Indonesia (56%). Only in Nigeria do Muslims express positive views of al-Qaeda; 49% have a favorable view and just 34% have an unfavorable view of bin Laden's organization.

Pew Research Center Global Attitudes Project
December 2010

his actions, and that Allah is on his side. We are left then with a world of two Islams.

Maior Islamic Terrorist Groups

About seventy major terrorist groups operate in the world. Of these, more than thirty are Islamic in orientation. Of the rest, only a few are widely recognized, like the Aum Shinrikyo group that spread poison gas in the Tokyo subway system. Among the Islamic groups, the most well known are:

- Abu Nidal Organization (aka Black September)
- Islamic Group or IG (aka Al-Gama'a al-Islamiyya)
- Armed Islamic Group
- Hamas
- Hizballah (Party of God, aka Islamic Jihad)
- al-Jihad (aka Islamic Jihad)
- al-Qaeda (of Osama bin Laden)

Before September 11, Americans for the most part were not worried about such groups. Europeans had a far greater sensitivity to terrorism because of militant groups operating in Ireland and Spain. Israel had first-hand experience with many Islamic terrorist groups. America seemed safe, even after the attacks on American embassies in Kenya and Tanzania, and on the USS Cole in South Yemen.

Some lecturers on terrorism have stated that there was more chance of dying from a fall in your bathtub than from a terrorist attack. As absurd as it sounds now, that point had merit prior to September's attack. The U.S. State Department lists a total of 77 American casualties in terrorist attacks around the world from 1995 through 2000, and then, on one day, nearly 3,000 died in the World Trade Center alone.

The Islamic terrorist groups have several aims: (1) use violence to bring their version of Islam to particular Muslim countries; (2) establish a Palestinian state; (3) destroy the State of Israel; (4) crush dissent against their views; and (5) attack the United States of America. These goals are expressed in the language of religious hatred. On Sunday, October 9, 2001 al-Jazeera satellite TV released a statement from Osama bin Laden that captures his style and ideology. Here are excerpts:

America is filled with fear. America has been filled with horror from north to south and east to west, and thanks be to God what America is tasting now is only a copy of what we have tasted. God has blessed a group of vanguard Muslims to destroy America and may God bless them and allot them a supreme place in heaven.

I swear to God that America will never dream of security or see it before we live it and see it in Palestine, and not before the infidels' armies leave the land of Muhammad, peace be upon him.

Of course, behind these words lie deeds of terror. Judith Miller reported from the Middle East for The New York Times for years and wrote about it in her book *God Has Ninety-Nine Names*. Her powerful prose captures the depth of tragedy and evil in militant Islam, whether in the Sudanese slave trade, the execution of moderates in Egypt, the slaughter of Kurdish Muslims in Iraq, the gangrape of devout Muslim women in Algeria by Muslim extremists, or the killings of journalists in the same country (eighteen in 1994 alone), some by decapitation.

In the year prior to September 11, Israel was the target of terrorism repeatedly. Suicide bombers attacked restaurants and busy shopping areas, killing and injuring dozens of citizens. In some instances, individual Jewish youths were shot or stoned to death near their homes. Terrorist groups claimed responsibility for some actions, but others appeared to be the work of lone assailants.

Understanding Islamic Terrorism

"How could they do it?" A year or so of planning, waiting in Florida, New Jersey or Maine—wherever—enjoying life in America, and then, the unimaginable: two planes into the World Trade Center, one into the Pentagon, and another brought down in a field in Pennsylvania. Our first response was a failure of imagination. This simply could not be happening. How could we understand it?

There are six different views of the events of September 11.

Mental Illness

In this view, the terrorists are crazy, mad, and insane. Nothing can explain what they did because their actions are outside any ordinary discourse of reason and sense. These deeds are irrational, beyond the understanding of any decent human being. These are monsters of insanity.

Evil

The terrorists are the embodiment of wickedness. Their behavior can only be explained on the grounds of hellish hate. These are people without conscience, who have no moral compass. They are fanatics whose hearts are darkened by their alliance with evil.

This interpretation must take serious note of the fact that the evil is done under the guise of good, in the name of Allah. This brings to mind the thesis of Phillip Hallie's book *The Paradox of Cruelty*: most evil is done with "good" intentions.

Terrorist Ideology

To Osama bin Laden and his colleagues, there is no mystery to understanding why September 11 happened. The United States deserved what it got. It is an enemy of Allah, opposed to Islam, and worthy of destruction. Islamic terrorists believe what they are doing is right. Hundreds of thousands of young Muslim boys are being taught daily in this ideology. It will be their only schooling, and they are not allowed to ask questions.

Islam-bashing

This view contends the killings on September 11 prove once and for all that Islam is the religion of the sword. On this view, all Muslims are terrorists and Islam is the chief cause of the wickedness. Based on this, some Americans have attacked Muslims at will. Members of the Sikh faith, a religion very distinct from Islam, have been attacked simply because their turbans reminded assailants of the ones worn by Taliban leaders. [see www.sikhspectrum.com].

America-blaming

From this interpretation, while the events of September 11 are wrong, America has created its own fate through its abuse of power,

Islamic Terrorist Organizations from
U.S. State Department List
November 24, 2010

1. Abu Nidal Organization (ANO)

2. Abu Sayyaf Group (ASG)

3. Al-Aqsa Martyrs Brigade (AAMS)

4. Al-Shabaab

5. Ansar al-Islam (AAI)

6. Asbat al-Ansar

7. Gama'a al-Islamiyya (Islamic Group)

8. HAMAS (Islamic Resistance Movement)

9. Harakat ul-Jihad-i-Islami/Bangladesh (HUJI-B)

10. Harakat ul-Mujahidin (HUM)

11. Hizballah (Party of God)

12. Islamic Jihad Union (IJU)

13. Islamic Movement of Uzbekistan (IMU)

14. Jaish-e-Mohammed (JEM) (Army of Mohammed)

15. Jemaah Islamiya organization (JI)

16. Kata'ib Hizballah (KH)

17. Kongra-Gel (KGK, formerly Kurdistan Workers' Party, PKK, KADEK)

18. Lashkar-e Tayyiba (LT) (Army of the Righteous)

19. Lashkar i Jhangvi (LJ)

20. Libyan Islamic Fighting Group (LIFG)

21. Moroccan Islamic Combatant Group (GICM)

22. Mujahedin-e Khalq Organization (MEK)

23. Palestine Liberation Front (PLF)

24. Palestinian Islamic Jihad (PIJ)

25. Popular Front for the Liberation of Palestine -General Command (PFLP-GC)

26. al-Qaeda in Iraq (AQI)

27. al-Qaeda (AQ)

28. al-Qaeda in the Arabian Peninsula (AQAP)

29. al-Qaeda in the Islamic Maghreb (formerly GSPC)

30. Harakat-ul Jihad Islami (HUJI)

31. Tehrik-e Taliban Pakistan (TTP)

32. Jundallah

its arrogance as the only reigning superpower, and its military attacks on Muslim people. Further, American complicity in the abuse of Palestinians by Israel has created legitimate anger toward the United States.

Failure in the Arab Muslim world

The attack on America is, according to this view, a result of a Muslim ignorance that lacks the will or freedom to be self-critical. The hatred of America is fueled by their jealousy of the wealth and freedom of America in contrast to the poverty and dictatorship in the Muslim Arab world. Thus, America is blamed for calamity, oppression, and evil that is actually caused by either the evil of Islamic dictatorships or the evil of Islamic militants.

This point has been articulated best by Kanan Makiya, author of the famous works *Republic of Fear* (on Saddam's Iraq) and *Cruelty and Silence*, a powerful protest against the silence of Arab intellectuals about the dark side of the militant Islamic Middle East. In a London Observer article, "Fighting Islam's Ku Klux Klan," Makiya writes of the incredible price that Muslims will pay if they "continue to wallow in the sense of one's own victimhood to the point of losing the essentially universal idea of human dignity and worth that is the only true measure of civility." [October 7, 2001]

He continues:

> Arabs and Muslims need today to face up to the fact that their resentment at America has long since become unmoored from any rational underpinnings it might once have had; like the anti-Semitism of the interwar years, it is today steeped in deeply embedded conspiratorial patterns of thought rooted in profound ignorance of how a society and a polity like the United States, much less Israel, functions.

His article ends with these words:

Support for al-Qaeda

So, the killing of these heroic chiefs doesn't—and won't—end the march of jihad (holy war), or extinguish its torch, or put out its light as the enemies imagine. Rather, their killing, in fact, pushes the march forward and strengthens, stabilizes, sharpens, and stimulates it.

Mustafa Abu al-Yazeed
Al-Qaeda's Afghanistan leader
On revenge for the death of Abu Laith al-Libi and other militants

Muslims and Arabs have to be on the front lines of a new kind of war, one that is worth waging for their own salvation and in their own souls. And that, as good out-of-fashion Muslim scholars will tell you, is the true meaning of jihad, a meaning that has been hijacked by terrorists and suicide bombers and all those who applaud or find excuses for them. To exorcise what they have done in our name is the civilisational challenge of the twenty-first century for every Arab and Muslim in the world today.

Islam: A Religion of Peace?

President George W. Bush has stated publicly on several occasions that "Islam is a religion of peace." By this he was making reference to the Islam that condemns terrorism, to the millions of Muslims who deplore Osama bin Laden, and to the significant Islamic traditions that support peace between religions and between all peoples. The president was speaking of the Islam that has brought meaning and stability to the lives of millions of its followers.

September 11 proved that there is another Islam, that of the Muslims who readily kill in the name of Allah. The terrorists who hijacked one of the planes at Logan Airport in Boston left behind

Fatwa against terrorism

The sanctity of human life and its protection occupies a fundamental place in Islamic law. Taking anyone's life for nothing is an act that is forbidden and unlawful. Rather, in some cases, it amounts to infidelity. These days, the terrorists, in a vain attempt to impose their own ideas and beliefs and eliminate their opponents from the face of the earth, killing innocent people ruthlessly and indiscriminately everywhere in mosques, bazaars, governmental offices, and other public places are in fact committing clear infidelity. They are warned of humiliating torment in this world and in the hereafter. Terrorism, in its very essence, is an act that symbolises infidelity and rejection of what Islam stands for.

His Eminence Shaykh-ul-Islam Dr Muhammad Tahir-ul-Qadri
February 2010

their instructions on what to do if a passenger interfered in their plot:

> If God grants any one of you a slaughter, you should perform it as an offering on behalf of your father and mother, for they are owed by you. Do not disagree among yourselves, but listen and obey. If you slaughter, you should plunder those you slaughter, for that is a sanctioned custom of the Prophet's.

When the president spoke of a peaceful Islam, Muslims of another stripe burned the American flag and dreamed of more attacks on America.

There is an Islam of peace. It is in the millions of Muslims who live every day in love and gentleness. It is in the Muslim praying five times a day for no more terrorist attacks. It is in those mosques where clerics preach that Islam is not a religion of the sword. It is in those Afghans who know that Osama bin Laden has betrayed their country. It is in those Muslims who know that there is a hateful perversion of "Islam" that could not possibly be from Allah, the all-Merciful Creator.

7

Palestine

Israel and Palestine

Understanding Islam in modern times demands knowledge of the Palestinian issue and the way conflict over Palestine has shaped the self-identity of Muslims throughout the world. Public dialogue since September 11 has often raised the Palestinian question as a factor in understanding, and even defending, Islamic extremism and the nature of terrorism.

Sixty Key Dates in the Palestinian Conflict

Since the rise of Zionism in the late 1800s, there have been increasing conflicts between Jews and Arabs in Palestine. Here are sixty key dates.

Timeline

1882 – First wave of Jewish immigration to Palestine

1896 – Theodore Herzl publishes *The Jewish State*

1897 – First International Zionist Congress is formed

1904 – Second wave of Jewish immigration occurs

1914 – World War I begins

1916 – Sykes-Picot agreement between Britain and France is signed

1917 – Balfour declaration is released in support of Jewish state

1919 – Third wave of Jewish immigration occurs

1920 – Lebanon separated from Syria by the French

1920 – Arab revolt takes place in Jerusalem (April)

1920 – Formation of Haganah (Jewish underground army) in Palestine

1924 – Fourth wave of Jewish immigration takes place

1929 – Massacre of Jews in Hebron (August)

1931 – Formation of the Irgun (Jewish underground militia) in Palestine

1933 – Hitler gains power in Germany

1933 – Fifth wave of Jewish immigration takes place

1936 – Peel Commission on Palestine mandate

1939 – World War II begins

1942 – Jewish Holocaust dominates Nazi plans

1946 – Irgun bombing of King David Hotel (July 22) in Palestine

1947 – Palestinias reject UN plan of partition

1948 – Massacre of Palestinians at Deir Yassin (April 9)

1948 – Proclamation of Jewish state (May 14)

1948 – War of Independence begins

1956 – Sinai War begins

1964 – Founding of the Palestinian Liberation Organization

1967 – Six-Day War begins (June 5–10)

1972 – Murder of Jewish Olympians in Munich (September 5)

1973 – Yom Kippur War (October)

1974 – Peace treaty signed between Jordan and Israel

1977 – Anwar Sadat, the president of Egypt, makes peace trip to Jerusalem (November 19)

1978 – Camp David Accord negotiated between Sadat and Begin (Prime Minister of Israel)

1979 – Revolution occurs in Iran under Ayatollah Khomeini

1981 – Egyptian President Sadat assassinated (October 6)

1982 – Israel invades Lebanon (June 6)

1982 – Massacre of Palestinians at Sabra and Shatilla (September 16–19)

1985 – *Achille Lauro* hijacked by Palestinian terrorists (October 7)

1987 – First Uprising (Intifadah) by Palestinian youth

1991 – Gulf War to liberate Kuwait

1991 – Middle East peace talks in Madrid

1993 – Oslo Peace Accords

1994 – Jordan recognizes State of Israel

1995 – Assassination of Yitzhak Rabin (November 4)

2000 – President Clinton fails to negotiate deal between Israel and Palestinians

2000 – Second Intifadah triggered by Ariel Sharon visiting the Dome of the Rock

2001 – Dramatic increase in suicide bombings in Israel

2001 – September 11 terrorist attacks in U.S.

2002 – Prime Minister Sharon sends army into Jenin

2002 – Proposal for peace by Saudi Crown Prince Abdullah

2002 – Israel approves security wall

2004 – Death of Arafat (November 11)

2005 – Mahmoud Abbas elected Palestinian Authority president

2005 – Israeli forces leave Gaza and the West Bank (August)

2006 – Hamas defeats Fatah in elections in Gaza (January)

2006 – Israeli-Lebanese war (July 12–August 14)

2007 – Fighting between Hamas and Fatah

2008 – Gaza under Israeli attack (December 27–January 19, 2009)

2009 – U.S. President Barak Obama speaks in Cairo

2010 – U.S. pushes for Israeli-Palestinian negotiations

2011 – Gaza Youth Manifesto for Change

Different Interpretations of the Palestinian Question

Studying the details of the history of the Palestinian question will leave anyone deeply depressed for several reasons. First, the conflict between Jews and Arabs has been one full of blood. There have been five major wars between Jews and Arabs in the half-century since the founding of the state of Israel in 1948.

Second, the history of the Palestinian conflict is one of missed opportunities. Things could have been different. Jews started to return to Palestine in the late 1800s. Throughout this 120-year period, certain choices were made by both Jews and Arabs that ensured further conflict. The wrong voices were heard. The will for peace died. The sword of revenge was taken up repeatedly.

Third, any student of Israeli or Palestinian history will see immediately that ideological divisions run so deep that it is almost impossible to imagine a decisive turn toward peace. This involves: (1) radical differences in religious views, (2) competing political understandings, (3) divergent historical verdicts, and (4) opposing moral views about every aspect of the conflict.

The differences of opinion about Israel and Palestine can be expressed in four competing interpretations. Understanding the nature and power of these four views is a necessary first step for any understanding of the complex and tragic story of the Jewish and Arab conflict of the Middle East, a conflict that affects Jews and Muslims everywhere.

The dominant Jewish position (written in the voice of the advocate)

The founding of the state of Israel is a moral and historical fact. Given the hatred Jews have encountered throughout history, and in the face of the Holocaust, the Jewish people had every right to re-create their homeland. This great victory for the world Jewish

Balfour Declaration of England 1917

His Majesty's Government views with favor the establishment in Palestine of a national home for the Jewish people, and will use their best endeavors to facilitate the achievement of this object, it being clearly understood that nothing shall be done which may prejudice the civil and religious rights of existing non-Jewish communities in Palestine or the rights and political status enjoyed by Jews in any other country.

community occurred on May 15, 1948. For the first time in two thousand years, we were home.

Tragically, the Arab world chose not to accept the proposal of the United Nations to have two separate states in Palestine. Instead, Arabs chose to fight Israel in 1948, and have done so ever since. The Arab world wants Israel to be destroyed. Four of the wars since independence in 1948 involved attack on Israel by Arabs, including Palestinians. Our invasion of Lebanon was a necessary measure to wipe out terrorist bases in that country.

Israel's aggression against the Palestinians is about legitimate self-defense. We cannot be at peace with a people who hate us, who want us destroyed. The world must not give nation status to a terrorist people. The Palestinian mind has been corrupted by decades of racist hate toward the Jew and toward Israel, a hatred fueled by Islamic militants throughout the world.

The events of September 11 have sadly brought to America what Israel has faced for years: the wanton killing of innocent people by terrorists driven by hate. We are grateful for the help of the United States in defending the freedom of Israel. You have been our strongest ally in our fight for survival. Together, we will stand strong against the forces that seek to destroy us.

We hope, of course, that Palestinians will stop their hatred of Israel, affirm our right to nationhood, and cease their terrorist activities against Jews in Israel and throughout the world. We are ready to negotiate with The Palestianian Authority at any time, providing that the Palestinians lay down their rocks and their bombs. Their continued war on Israel shows their obsession with the destruction of our nation. We will not be moved.

The moderate Jewish position (written in the voice of the advocate)

The birth of Israel is a joy to all Jews. It is a miracle from God who brought us back to our land. But with this incredible gift comes enormous moral and spiritual responsibility. We cannot allow the forces of anti-Semitism to blind us to commitment to the ideals that have been our beacon of light through the centuries as a people with no land.

There is much in the birth of Israel that stains our purity. From the start, and through the last century, we gave no serious moral thought to the rights and needs of the Arabs who were already here when we started to come home. Menachim Begin, who later became prime minister, even engaged in terrorist acts against the British in the mid-1940s. We secretly conspired against Arabs even as we publicly said we wanted Palestinians to have their own state.

While there is no excuse for the Arab attacks on our nation, there is also no justification for what we have done to the Palestinians. Our invasion of Lebanon in 1982 was an unjust attack on another nation. The Palestinians have a right to their own country. We must overcome our own bigotry and hatred.

We are becoming a terrorist nation against the Palestinians. Our secret defense forces have blown up Palestinian militia headquarters. We have destroyed Palestinian homes. We have razed entire villages. Our soldiers have engaged in torture of Palestinians. We have our hired assassins. We have our own zealots who match Islamic terrorists word for word, deed for deed. All of this must stop.

The extreme Palestinian position (written in the voice of the advocate)

Palestine has been a home of Arabs for hundreds of years. We lost our native land through Zionist aggression. We refused the United Nations' partition of our land because it was our land. The British dominated us by force and they left us to the Zionist Jews to do the same. Our country was stolen from us by the Jewish pig.

We were attacked by the Jews throughout the twentieth century. We engaged in jihad against them on four occasions because it is our duty to cleanse the earth of their filth. We will not stop until the Jews are forced into the ocean. The American fascists support Israel because America is run by Jews. The Jew runs the economies of the world, including Britain, Germany, and Japan.

The Jews use the lie of the Holocaust to create sympathy for their cause. Hitler opposed the Jew for the same reason we do: the Jewish vermin will poison and destroy everything in their path. The Jews have even published their plans to run the world. Their leaders met and reported of their attempted conquest in their Protocols of the Elders of Zion.

The attack on the World Trade Center is probably a Zionist plot, cooked up by the American CIA in bed with the Israeli Mossad. If it is the work of Osama bin Laden, well, American Jewry is getting what it deserves. Either way, it is really the fault of the Jew. Jews were told to stay home from the World Trade Center on that day. They will never stop oppressing us because they have always stood against Allah and his true followers.

The Jewish leaders of Israel assault our holy places. They humiliate us at their checkpoints. They raid our lands and burn down our villages. They kill our leaders, rape our women, maim our children, torture our soldiers. They cut off our water supplies, keep us from work, shut down our schools, and grind us into poverty. Allah will inflict upon them the fires of eternal hell.

The moderate Palestinian position (written in the voice of the advocate)

It is a historical fact that we were here long before the Jews arrived in 1882. We have a moral right to nationhood. However, our path to freedom demands that we recognize the nation of Israel. Whether we like it or not, Israel is here to stay. We must stop our hatred of Jews and our talk of wiping Israel off the map. We made a terrible error when we refused the U.N. offer of statehood in 1947.

We have engaged in brutal acts against innocent Israelis. Every terrorist act has dulled whatever inclination Israel may have to grant us our own country. We have been our own worst enemies. We will not gain the international support we need until we stop our quest for blood. Osama bin Laden has hurt our cause and has brought great shame to Islam. We must not follow in his path.

We have been racists against Israel. We have trusted anti-Semitic lies about Jews, including the bizarre theory that the Holocaust never happened. We stereotype Jews much like the rest of the world draws stereotypes of us. We will never learn to get along until we stop our bigotry and our hate. The throwing of stones must stop. Our bombing must stop.

Following the way of Allah means we must be people of peace. Muhammad (Peace Be Upon Him) taught us that war is to be used only as a last resort. Many Jews of good will (People of the Book) know that we deserve our own land. It is time for our elected leaders to deal in good faith with Jewish leaders. The tragic events of September 11 show us that terror just breeds more terror. For the sake of our children, all children, let us return to the table of peace.

Responding to the Views

Anyone with any emotion and common sense will know that these views represent different universes. However, we cannot let that fact leave us in despair that no progress can be made. So let me suggest some essentials in a proper response.

These four views are not an exhaustive look at the Palestinian question. For example, the reader might note the absence of a racist Jewish view that is parallel to the extreme Palestinian position. There are, however, examples. One extremist Jewish view is the circulated material and views propounded by a Jewish terrorist group founded by Rabbi Meir Kahane, the victim of an assassin's bullet in November 1990.

It may be hard for many readers to imagine that some Muslims employ such racist language about Jews. Tragically, Muslims have duplicated some Christian anti-Semitism as well as some of the views propogated in Germany during and prior to World War II. The extreme Palestinian view is real, and it is as popular as Hitler's was seventy-five years ago. Some Muslims have the same view of the Jews that Hitler did.

In fact, Jeffrey Goldberg wrote an article on Islamic extremism for the *New Yorker* magazine [October 8, 2001] where he quotes a Muslim cleric from Egypt who had this to say:

> Thanks to Hitler, of blessed memory, who on behalf of the Palestinians took revenge in advance, against the most vile criminals on the face of the earth. Although we do have a complaint against him, for his revenge was not enough.

This is beyond vile.

No amount of racism will undo the proof that the Holocaust is a real event in history. The evidence about Hitler's attempted extermination of the Jews is overwhelming except to the morally

Declaration of the State of Israel May 14, 1948

Accordingly we, members of the People's Council, representatives of the Jewish community of Eretz-Israel and of the Zionist movement, are here assembled on the day of the termination of the British Mandate over Eretz-Israel and, by virtue of our natural and historic right and on the strength of the resolution of the United Nations General Assembly, hereby declare the establishment of a Jewish State in Eretz-Israel, to be known as the State of Israel.

THE STATE OF ISRAEL will be open for Jewish immigration and for the Ingathering of the Exiles; it will foster the development of the country for the benefit of all its inhabitants; it will be based on freedom, justice and peace as envisaged by the prophets of Israel; it will ensure complete equality of social and political rights to all its inhabitants irrespective of religion, race or sex; it will guarantee freedom of religion, conscience, language, education and culture; it will safeguard the Holy Places of all religions; and it will be faithful to the principles of the Charter of the United Nations.

blind. The case for a Palestinian state is hurt by the prevalence of Holocaust denial or by conspiracy theories against Israel.

There is a great chasm, virtually unbridgeable, between extreme Jewish and Muslim views on Palestine. The divide between a moderate Palestinian approach and even the dominant Jewish position is less significant. It is out of the middle ground of the moderate positions that peace has the best opportunity. But, for both Arab and Jew, it will not be peace at any price.

What stands in the way of peace is that the violence on both sides is rooted in a hardness of heart that refuses to acknowledge that the "other" (whether Jew or Arab) is to be treated differently than this view of violence allows. Neither extreme wants to give ground by admitting fault, showing weakness, granting that the situation is complex, or by sharing guilt to any extent.

Many readers may be shocked by the moderate Jewish view, since it raises disturbing charges about Israel's treatment of the Palestinians. Many in the West automatically give Israel a presumption of innocence. Evangelical Christians, who believe that all Jews should trust Jesus as Messiah, often argue that criticism of Israel is against God's will.

The case for Israel must not be based in the kind of zealous ideology that shows no regard for facts or openness to evidence. We must examine charges against Israel one by one, simply out of a concern for truth and justice. If Israel's policy about Palestine is fundamentally right, it will not crumble with this or that admission of fault, unless of course the evidence of Israeli guilt becomes overwhelming.

In the last fifteen years, the case for a Palestinian state has grown more popular among moderate Jews and many observers who are very sympathetic to Israel. Hans Küng, the great Christian theologian of Germany, wrote after the Gulf War in *Judaism: Between Yesterday and Tomorrow*:

> The devastating consequences of the policy of occupation, including the moral consequences, are becoming increasingly clear to many Israelis. And as one who has so openly attacked the silence of Pius XII and the German bishops over the Jewish question, I may not keep silent over what Israelis are doing over the Palestinian question [p. 539].

Küng's concerns have been echoed by Jewish writers. Amos Oz wrote in an editorial for The New York Times:

> With or without Islamic fundamentalism, with or without Arab terrorism, there is no justification whatsoever for the lasting occupation and suppression of the Palestinian people by Israel. We have no right to deny Palestinians their natural right to self-determination.

He continues:

The occupation of the West Bank and Gaza by Israel has not made Israel secure—on the contrary, it makes our self-defense much harder and more complicated. The sooner this occupation ends, the better it will be for Palestinians and Israelis alike. [*New York Times*, September 14, 2001].

The same point has been made most powerfully by Michael Lerner, the editor of *Tikkun* magazine, and one of America's leading liberal Jewish activists. Lerner has received numerous death threats for his advocacy of a Palestinian state. However, his defense of the right of Palestinians to a homeland is in the context of strong denunciation of their terrorist attacks on Israel and the need for Palestinians to renounce their hatred of Jews.

8

A Christian Response to Islam

Engaging Muslims sometimes involves a critique of Islam. Since 9/11 it bears repeating that Christian witness to Islam should focus more on the positive news of the gospel and less on weaknesses in Islam. Affirmation about Jesus is always more important and usually more helpful than negative critique of another religious leader or non-Christian path. When a critique is necessary, Christians should speak with respect and love in order to increase the effectiveness of witnessing about the full revelation of God in Jesus Christ.

Jesus, Son of God

The core of Christian faith involves recognition of Jesus as the Son of God. As noted earlier, Islam fails to recognize that Jesus is divine and instead acknowledges Jesus as merely a prophet. Islam cannot be considered a revelation from God given this failure to recognize an essential element of God's revelation about Jesus. This error alone constitutes sufficient reason for abandoning any notion that Muhammad was a prophet of God.

Of course, like many non-Christians, Muslims misunderstand the doctrine of Trinity. Muslims have sometimes been taught that belief in Jesus as the Son of God means that Jesus is a biological son of God and Mary. Christians must explain that the Trinity does not mean three gods but that God is one God in three persons. The triune understanding of God is rooted in the New Testament. Early Christians held to the divinity of Jesus. Jesus is described with the titles of Jehovah; he is called the Son of God, and he is even addressed as God (eg., John 1:1; 8:58) On these matters, see Murray Harris, *Jesus as God* (Baker, 1998). Of course, Christians should recognize that the nature of the Trinity is beyond human understanding.

The Death of Jesus

Islam also denies the cornerstone of Christian faith that Jesus died on the cross. The Islamic teaching that Jesus was replaced on the cross by Judas (or some other figure) contradicts the ancient historical record found in all four Gospels, and the explicit teaching in Acts, and the rest of the New Testament. The one or two Quranic verses (4:157–158) that deny the death of Jesus are written six hundred years after his death, hardly a great source for historical accuracy about Jesus.

The Bible

On a broader level, Christians must recognize that the Bible is very different from the Quran. Many biblical stories and teachings, found throughout Scripture differ from the stories in the Quran. Further, some of the traditions in the Quran reflect later post-biblical Jewish and Christian misunderstandings of biblical material.

Though the Quran contains some teachings in harmony with Christian faith and with Old Testament tradition, the differences make it impossible to believe that the Quran is a product of divine revelation.

Muhammad

Christians must also express serious reservations about the prophetic authority of Muhammad. The teachings of Jesus Christ and those of the Holy Spirit through the New Testament writers alone are authoritative. This does not mean that Muhammad is the total embodiment of evil. However, Muhammad's life reads more like that of Moses or David, as if we were taken back to the warrior motifs of the Old Testament. This is not that surprising given that the Arabia of Muhammad's day was a land of tribal warfare. Further, the hadith material about Muhammad must be questioned at key points in relation to both historical reliability and the moral credibility of the prophet and his community of faith.

Here, it is important to give a word of caution. Most Muslims find it very offensive to hear or read criticism of their prophet. Christians need to think how it feels when someone attacks Jesus. Points of concern about Muhammad must be presented respectfully and at the right time. This is not about minimizing free speech but about maximizing wise use of knowledge.

Salvation

Because faith in Jesus' death alone is humanity's salvation, Christians must reject the Islamic concept of salvation. Islam emphasizes law and obedience to God as the way of salvation. As well, the Quran says that it is God in his sovereign will who decides who is saved or not. The dual emphasis on works righteousness and God's sovereignty leads many Muslims to have a lack of assurance about salvation. Christians, on the other hand, trust in salvation by faith and grace alone through Christ.

Women

The treatment of women in many Islamic countries and families must remain a matter of concern. Though Christian tradition contains some nasty teaching on and treatment of women (some Christian groups today still oppress women), there is no excuse for ignoring the contemporary plight of women in many Muslim countries. Many Muslim women in non-Western countries have little access to the freedoms taken for granted by Muslim females in the West. This is illustrated, for example, in the 2009 *Globe and Mail* interviews of Muslim women in Kandahar, Afghanistan.

Human Rights

The overall lack of human rights and freedom under Islamic law must continue to be the object of Christian critique. Christians must work with moderate Muslims to help further the cause of human rights. This applies to the issue of death for apostates under all schools of Islamic law. It also includes the lack of religious freedom for non-Muslims in Islamic countries and for Muslims who are Sunni in Shi'ite countries, or Shi'ite in Sunni countries

Christian-Muslim Relations

Relations today between Muslims and Christians are marred by the realities of war and the terrorist threat. The Palestinian-Israeli conflict also looms largely in Christian-Muslim relations as well as Christian relations with Palestinian Christians. On December 3, 2010 Hamas' Al-Aqsa TV ran a sermon which implored: "Allah, strike the Jews and their sympathizers, the Christians and their supporters. Allah, count them and kill them to the last one, and don't leave even one." Such provocations from Hamas and other radical Islamic groups are real and relatively common.

However, these statements from radicals must not be interpreted to suggest that all Muslims condone such violence and hatred. This is seen most clearly in the declaration *A Common Word between Us and You*, issued by 138 prominent Muslim leaders in 2007. It appeals for greater Christian-Muslim dedication to peace:

> So let our differences not cause hatred and strife between us. Let us vie with each other only in righteousness and good works. Let us respect each other, be fair, just and kind to another and live in sincere peace, harmony and mutual goodwill.

Christian leaders at the Yale Center for Faith and Culture responded with a reciprocal document titled *Loving God and Neighbor Together*.

The socio-political dynamics involved in Christian-Muslim relations needs emphasis, especially on two fronts. First, millions of Muslims live under either harsh dictatorships and/or oppressive financial conditions. Both of these realities limit the freedom Muslims have to hear the Gospel. Second, Christians also need to recognize the fact that most Muslims link Christian faith to the actions of the United States and other western powers. This has an enormous impact on the hearing of the Gospel.

That is why Christian leaders must constantly emphasize a Jesus-centered approach, not a political one. The Grace and Truth Affirmation notes: "We affirm a Jesus-centered approach to Muslims because it highlights the treasure of the gospel. It does not confuse the good news with Christendom, patriotism, or our civilization." This will provide opportunity for Christian-Muslim dialogue and for Christians to present Muslims with a better understanding of the person, work, and teachings of Jesus. Muslims need to be aware of the proper identity of Jesus, the reality of his death and resurrection, and the God-given path of salvation in Jesus.

9

Now What?

For the near future, attempts to understand Islam will continue to be made in relation to September 11. That day is now marked in history in the same way as November 22, the day President John Kennedy died, and December 7, the attack on Pearl Harbor. In many ways it represents a turning point in the affairs of humanity.

Where we go from here depends on how the world continues to respond to the events of that fateful day and what they represent. As with any epochal global tragedy, September 11 can continue to be a spark that ignites even greater tragedy, or it can continue to stir all mankind to consciously turn from hatred and terror toward international understanding and peace.

How have Muslims responded to 9/11? Thankfully, as we have seen, many Muslim scholars immediately condemned the terrorist distortion of Islam, and people around the world—including Islamic nations—expressed their sympathy and support for the victims of September 11. At the same time, militant Muslims celebrated the chaos in New York and Washington, and, as we know too well, terrorist attacks have continued in many nations.

As noted throughout this book, speaking broadly there are two very different kinds of Muslims. There is one group that admires, defends, and supports the work of international terrorism in the name of Allah. The other, much larger group sees the actions of September 11 as a betrayal of Islam, the Prophet, and the Quran. Only time will reveal which view will carry the day.

On September 20, 2001, President Bush made the distinction between the two types of Muslims clear in his address to the joint session of Congress:

> I also want to speak tonight directly to Muslims throughout the world. We respect your faith. It's practiced freely by many millions of Americans and by millions more in countries that America counts as friends. Its teachings are good and peaceful, and those who commit evil in the name of Allah blaspheme the name of Allah. The terrorists are traitors to their own faith, trying, in effect, to hijack Islam itself. The enemy of America is not our many Muslim friends; it is not our many Arab friends. Our enemy is a radical network of terrorists, and every government that supports them.

Events of September 11 and all similar acts force humanity to decide which of the paths ahead humankind should choose. It is not inevitable that the evils of that day or any other have to lead to other evils, or be the opening salvo into greater and greater cycles of terror. Humans, individually and collectively, can choose paths of goodness and peace because we have seen evil and do not want to go there anymore.

The peace that could emerge from Ground Zero will be hard to reach, since the enemies of peace are so powerful, and hate is so deep in those who know nothing but terror's awful pull, especially a terror disguised in the name of God. The path to global peace demands the engagement of all people of good will against militant Islam and, of course, against other evils that oppress humanity. This cause for peace must unite our planet, whether we are religious, atheist, or agnostic. September 11 demands a renewed determination to love justice, goodness, and peace so much that earth becomes a safer, more harmonious place.

The events of that terrible day demand a striving for real peace among all religious people of good will. September 11 was an act of evil carried out in the name of religion. It must be met by a billion acts of goodness by religious people. This is not to suggest that all religions are the same, but that religious people share common values.

What is needed is what Hans Küng argued at two Parliaments of the World Religions: there will be no peace until there is peace between religions. He is not advocating some cheap agreement between faiths or simplistic reactions to real, complex problems. Rather, we must seek a deep, worldwide commitment to the paths of goodness taught by Christianity, Islam, and all major religions.

Since September 11, there have been countless editorials and many books about the true nature of Islam. This difference of opinion has been predictable, but one that is important and necessary. These differences of opinion range between, "yes, Osama bin Laden and the Taliban are true Muslims, and they show us what Islam is really like," and, "no, Islam is a religion of peace; bin Laden and the Taliban extremists are really a product of a militant fascism that has nothing to do with Muhammad or the Quran." One can hope and work for a world where more and more Muslims choose a path of peace. It is up to them, of course, but not just them.

Appendix A

Key Dates

632	Death of Muhammad
633	Muslim forces enter Syria
634	Death of Abu Bakr, the first *caliph* or successor to Muhammad
636	Battle of Yarmuk (Muslim control over Syria)
636	Battle of al-Qadisyyah (Muslim conquest of modern-day Iraq)
637	Capture of Jerusalem by Muslim leaders
641	Alexandria conquered by Muslim force then regained by Byzantine fleet
645	Muslims retake Alexandria
652	Muslim attack on Sicily fails
653	Fall of Cyprus
661	Assassination of Ali, the fourth *caliph* to Muhammad
667	Muslim attack on Sicily fails
672	Fall of Rhodes
680	Murder of Husayn, grandson of the Prophet
690	Construction of the Dome of the Rock in Jerusalem
705	Carthage razed by Muslims

711	Tareq ibn Zaid invades Spain
720	Muslim attack on Sicily fails
728	Death of Hasan al-Basri, early spiritual leader
732	Muslims defeated at Battle of Tours (Charles Martel)
750	Rise of the Abbasid Dynasty, based in Baghdad
765	Split among Shi'ite Muslims over new leader
767	Death of Abu Hanifah (leading jurist for Indian and Middle East Muslims)
809	Fall of Sardinia
818	Fall of Majorca
824	Fall of Crete
831	Fall of Palermo
835	Fall of Malta
850	Death of al-Bukhari, specialist on Islamic *hadith*
851	Martyrdom of Christians at Cordova by Muslims
855	Death of Ahmad ibn Hanbal (b. 780)
871	Fall of Syracuse
902	Fall of Taormina
940	Twelfth Shi'a Imam becomes the "hidden imam"
950	Death of Al-Farabi, the Muslim Aristotle
975	Founding of Al-Azhar university in Cairo
1017	Mahmud of Ghazni (d. 1030) plunders north India
1037	Death of Ibn Sina (aka Avicenna), a great Islamic philosopher
1085	Fall of Toledo
1094	El Cid conquered Valencia
1095	Start of First Crusade by Pope Urban II
1098	Fall of Antioch to Crusaders (June 3)

1099	Crusaders capture Jerusalem (July 15)
1111	Death of al-Ghazali
1118	Hugh of Payns created Templars
1128	In Praise of the New Chivalry (Bernard of Clairvaux)
1144	Zengi captures Edessa
1145	Eugenius III launches Second Crusade with *Quantum Praedecessores*
1146	Bernard of Clairvaux promotes Crusade
1154	Nur ad-Din took Damascus
1185	Saladin makes treaty with Byzantine
1187	Saladin won Battle of Hattin (July 4) and captured Jerusalem (Oct. 2)
1191	Battle of Arsuf (Richard vs. Saladin) Third Crusade
1198	Fourth Crusade called by Innocent III
1202	Zara sacked by Crusaders
1204	Western Crusaders sack Constantinople
1208	Albigensian Crusade called by Innocent III
1212	Battle of Las Navas de Tolosa
1215	Fifth Crusade called in Ad liberandam during Fourth Lateran Council
1219	St. Francis meets with al-Kamil during Crusade
1221	Crusaders surrender in Nile Delta
1229	Frederick II captures Jerusalem (Sixth Crusade) February
1248	King Louis IX departed for East during Seventh Crusade
1258	Mongols sack Baghdad
1273	Death of Rumi (b. 1207)
1291	Fall of Acre
1295	Mongol dynasty converts to Islam
1300	Rise of Ottoman Empire

1307	Templars suppressed by King Philip IV
1315	Death of Raymond Lull, Christian missionary to Muslims
1356	Alexandria sacked by Peter I of Cyprus
1389	Ottomans defeat Balkan allies at Battle of Kosovo
1426	Cyprus under Egyptian control
1453	Ottomans capture Constantinople and rename it Istanbul
1478	Start of Spanish Inquisition
1492	End of Muslim rule in Spain
1492	Fall of Granada
1517	Salim I (Ottoman) conquers Egypt
1520	Rise of Suleiman the Magnificent, the Ottoman emperor
1526	Muslim armies under Babur enter India
1563	Akbar gains power in India
1566	Death of Suleiman
1683	Ottoman forces defeated at Battle of Vienna
1796	Treaty of Tripoli
1798	Napoleon in Egypt
1803	Wahhabi movement gains control in Saudi Arabia
1830	France occupies Algeria
1881	British take control of Egypt
1893	Alexander Russell Webb at World's Parliament of Religions (Chicago)
1897	First Zionist Congress (Basle)
1902	Qasim Amin pioneers feminism in Egypt
1910	Oil prospects in Persia
1914	Start of World War I (August 4)
1915	British and French forces defeated at Gallipoli (April)

1915	Beginning of Armenian genocide
1916	Arab revolt led by Sharif Hussein against Ottoman rule
1916	Sykes-Picot agreement between Britain and France
1917	Balfour Declaration (November)
1920	San Remo conference
1920	Lebanon separated from Syria by French
1920	Arab revolts in Jerusalem (April)
1920	Formation of the Haganah (Jewish underground militia)
1923	Turkey becomes republic under Mustafa Kemal Atatürk
1925	Abdul Aziz ibn Saud captures Mecca from Sharif Hussein
1928	Muslim Brotherhood founded by Hassan al-Banna
1929	Jews killed by Arabs at Hebron (August)
1931	Formation of the Irgun
1932	Political independence in Iraq
1936	Arab revolt in Palestine led by Haj Amin Al-Husseini
1936	Peel Commission on Palestine mandate (report: 1937)
1939	Start of World War II (September 3)
1941	Mohammad Reza Pahlavi becomes Shah of Iran
1946	Syria gains independence from France
1946	Irgun bombing of King David Hotel (July 22)
1947	Creation of Pakistan
1948	Jewish attack on Deir Yassan (April 9)
1948	Founding of the State of Israel (May 14)
1949	Hassan al-Banna assassinated
1952	Nasser leads coup in Egypt
1953	CIA aids coup against Iranian leader Mohammad Mosaddeq

1954	Algerian war of independence begins
1955	Sudan gains independence from British-French rule
1956	Suez Canal crisis
1962	Algeria gains independence
1964	Formation of the Palestinian Liberation Organization
1965	Assassination of Malcolm X in New York City
1966	Sayyid Qutb executed in Egypt (August 29)
1967	Six-Day War between Israel and Egypt (June 5–10)
1969	Qaddafi stages coup in Libya
1970	Death of Egypt president Nasser (September 28)
1972	"Black September" attack on Israeli Olympic athletes (September 5)
1973	October War between Israel and Arabs
1974	Peace treaty between Jordan and Israel
1975	Start of civil war in Lebanon
1977	Anwar Sadat makes historic peace trip to Jerusalem (November 19)
1978	Saddam Hussein controls Baath party in Iraq
1979	Islamic revolution in Iran under Khomeini (February)
1979	USSR invades Afghanistan
1979	Iranian hostage crisis (November 4)
1980	Iran-Iraq War (September 22, 1980–August 20, 1988)
1981	Release of U.S. hostages in Iran (January 20)
1981	Israel destroys nuclear reactor in Iraq (June 7)
1981	Assassination of Anwar Sadat (October 6)
1981	Universal Islamic Declaration of Human Rights
1982	Syrian army massacres Muslim Brothers in Hama (February)
1982	Israeli invasion of Lebanon (June 6)

1982	Massacre at Sabra and Shatila camps in Beirut (September 16–19)
1983	Attack on U.S. and French soldiers in Beirut (October 23)
1985	Palestinian terrorists hijack *Achille Lauro* (October 7)
1987	Intifada begins in Palestine
1988	Pan Am flight 103 blown up over Lockerbie, Scotland
1989	Iranian *fatwa* against Salman Rushdie for *The Satanic Verses*
1991	Gulf War to liberate Kuwait
1991	Military conflicts begin in former Yugoslavia
1992	Seige of Sarajevo begins (April 1992–February 1996)
1993	Bombing of the World Trade Center (February 26)
1993	Oslo Accords (Washington signing September 13)
1994	Jordan recognizes State of Israel
1995	Massacre in Srebrenica (July)
1995	Assassination of Yitzhak Rabin (November 4)
1996	Osama bin Laden announces Jihad against the U.S.
1996	Taliban take control of Kabul
1997	Collapse of Albania
1998	World Islamic Front issues Declaration against the U.S. (February 23)
1998	U.S. embassies in Kenya and Tanzania bombed (August 7)
1999	War in Kosovo
2000	Vatican issues Lenten apology
2000	Breakdown of President Clinton's Israel-Palestine peace talks
2000	*USS Cole* attacked in Yemen (October 12)
2001	September 11 terrorist attack on America
2001	Defeat of Taliban in Afghanistan
2002	Heightened suicide bombings in Israel

2002	Israel government approves security wall
2002	Terrorist bombing in Bali kills 202 (October 12)
2003	U.S. attacks Iraq (March)
2004	Crisis in Darfur escalates
2004	Madrid train bombings (March 11)
2004	Killing of Dutch filmmaker Theo van Gogh (November 2)
2004	Death of Arafat (November 11)
2005	Mahmoud Abbas elected Palestinian leader
2005	Rafik Hariri killed in Beirut (February 14)
2005	London bombings (July 7)
2005	Israeli forces leave Gaza and West Bank (August)
2005	Danish cartoon controversy erupts (September–December)
2006	Hamas defeats Fatah in general election (January)
2006	Arrest of suspected terrorists in Toronto (June 3)
2006	Israeli-Lebanese war (July 12–August 14)
2006	Pope Benedict XVI controversy (September)
2007	Fighting between Hamas and Fatah in Gaza
2007	Muslim and Christian leaders start new dialogue
2008	Gaza under Israeli attack (December 27–January 19, 2009)
2009	President Obama Speech in Cairo (June 4)
2010	Negotiations on Israel-Palestinian conflict
2010	Controversy over mosque proposal at Ground Zero
2010	Florida pastor threatens Quran burning
2011	Referendum on southern Sudan
2011	Revolutions in Tunisia and Egypt

Glossary

A.H.—After Hijrah (the expulsion of Muhammad to Medina in AD 622), starting point in Muslim calendar

Alim—a scholar or expert in Islam

Allahu Akbar—means "God is the greatest"; used in Islamic prayers.

Assalamu alaikum—Muslim greeting: "Peace be upon you"

Ayah (pl. ayat)—1. miracle or sign from God. 2. Each verse of the Quran

Ayatollah—highest-ranking religious leaders in Shia branch of Islam

Barakallah—means "May the blessing of Allah be upon you'

Bismillahir rahmanir—phrase from the Quran that means "In the name of Allah, the Most Beneficent, the Most Merciful."

Caliph or Khalifah—refers both to Muhammad's successors and to leaders of Islam in general

Dar al-islam—Abode of Islam—territory under Islamic rule

Dar ar-harb—Abode of war—territory outside Islamic control

Da'wah—mission of spreading Islam, evangelization

Dhimmi—non-Muslims living under Islamic control or law

Din—way of religion, way of life

Du'a-a prayer

Dunya—this life, this world

Eid—celebration or feast

Faqih—an expert or scholar in Islamic law or jurisprudence

Fard—anything that is obligatory, like praying five times per day

Fatihah—opening chapter of the Quran, recited in prayers

Fatwa—opinion or ruling in Islamic law

Fiqh—understanding and comprehension of Islamic law

Ghazi—term for soldier or warrior

Hadith—traditions about the prophet Muhammad

Hajj—the pilgrimmage to Mecca, one of the five pillars of Islam

Halal—something lawful or permitted, as in Halal food

Haraam—that which is illegal or not allowed in Islam

Haram—sanctuary or sacred territory, as in the haram of wives

Hijrah—refers to Muhammad's trip to Medina in AD 622 and is the first year of Islamic calendar (AH)

Iblis—Quranic word for Satan

Ijma—consensus in Islamic legal opinion

Imam—1. refers to spiritual or community leader in Islam. 2. The person who leads prayer. 3. In Shia Islam it refers to one of the early special leaders after Muhammad's death

Iman—trust, faith in Allah

Injil—the revelations given to the prophet Jesus (who is called Isa in Islam)

Isa—Jesus

In sha'allah—means "If Allah wills" or "If Allah permits"

Istighfar—to ask for divine forgiveness

Jahannam—hell

Jahiliyyah—the state of ignorance and disobedience in Arabia before the Prophet arrived to give truth

Jihad—1. to strive, to endeavor. 2. To engage in just war to defend Islam

Jinn—invisible spirit beings created by Allah, who can do good and bad just like humans

Jizyah—the tax paid by non-Muslims in an Islamic country

Jannah—paradise, heaven

Kaaba, Kabah, or Kaba—shrine or house of worship in the great mosque of Mecca that Muslims believe was built by Abraham

Kafir—an unbeliever, someone who rejects Allah and hisway

Kalam—Islamic logic and philosophy; can also mean speech

Khutbah—sermon or speech, used of sermon at Friday prayers

Laat—a major goddess figure in pre-Islamic Arabia

La ilaha Illallah—means "There is no God but Allah"-first part of confession of faith necessary to be a Muslim

Mahdi—a term in various divisions of Shia Islam for either the seventh or twelfth ruler who went into a state of hiding and is expected back at the end of time

Masjid—house of worship (mosque in English)

Miraj—when Muhammad was taken to heaven by the angel Gabriel

Mufti—an expert in Muslim law

Mujahid—a fighter for Islam (both literally and figuratively)

Mushrik—someone who believes in more than one God

Munafiq—a hypocrite or deceiver

Nabi—a prophet or messenger from God

PBUH—abbreviation for Peace Be Upon Him, said after reference is made to Muhammad

Qiblah—direction Muslims face when they pray to Mecca

Quraysh—Muhammad's tribe, the most powerful in Arabia

Ramadan—month in Muslim calendar when revelations were first given to Muhammad and month when Muslims fast

Rasul—messenger or prophet

Salah—pillar of special communion or prayer five times per day

SAW—abbreviation of "Salla Allahu 'Alaihi Wa Sallam," which means "May the Blessing of Allah be upon Him" and is to be said or written when reference is made to Muhammad

Sawm—pillar of total fasting during Ramadan

Shahadah—first pillar of confession: "There is no God but Allah, and Muhammad is His prophet."

Shaikh (or Sheikh)—religious leader or wise person in Islam; also elderly person

Shari'ah—the rules or laws of Islam

Shirk—the most serious offense of idol worship, teaching that God has partners, or putting something ahead of Allah

Sunnah—the life and deeds or way of Muhammad

Surah (pl. suwar)—refers to the chapter divisions of the Quran

Taqwa—the reverence or fear of Allah that leads to obedience

Tawaf—ritual of going around the Kabah seven times during pilgrimmage to Mecca

Ummah—the community of believers in Allah

Uzzah—major goddess worshipped in pre-Islamic Arabia

Wudu—washing or purification that is to take place before prayers

Zakat (or Zakah)—the pillar of giving a percent of wealth for the needy

Frequently Asked Questions About Islam

1. Is the Quran the same as the Koran?

   Yes. Koran is the older English word that is now usually obsolete among scholars. To be absolutely technical, most correct rendering of the Arabic into English is Qur'an.

2. Is Mohammed the same as Muhammad?

   Yes. These are simply two different English spellings for the Arabic word for Muhammad but they refer to the same person.

3. Do Muslims like to be called Muhammadans?

   No. They really dislike the term since they claim to be followers of Allah, not Muhammad. Though they hold Muhammad in the highest regard, he is not divine.

4. Can the Quran be understood in English?

   Yes, though even in Arabic the Quran is not written in a very orderly manner. The English translations lose the beauty of the Arabic, but they are faithful to the original language, especially the translation by A. J. Arberry.

5. Is Islam a religion of the sword?

   Yes, to some degree. Muhammad engaged in military battles against his enemies and Muslim leaders created a vast empire through war. However, while Muslims believe in just war, the Quran forbids using force to convert people.

6. Did Muhammad really believe what he taught?

   Yes. Critics of Muhammad who argue that he was a fraud pay little attention to the enormous evidence of his total commitment to his religion. He actually fought in military battle to defend his faith, something hard to imagine if he was a con artist.

7. Do Muslims have anything comparable to the Christian conversion experience?

   Yes, in a sense. Islam teaches that everyone is born a Muslim by being a creation of Allah. Conversion to Islam is explained as reversion to the original faith of their birth. Some who revert to Islam have very dramatic conversion stories.

8. Do Muslims believe that they can go to heaven if they do not make the pilgrimage to Mecca?

   All Muslims must make the pilgrimage if health and finances permit. To refuse to go to Mecca is a very grave and serious offense against Allah's law.

9. When Muslims pray, do they just recite phrases they have been taught, or do they pray from the heart?

   Prayers by Muslims are often recited, as during the five prayer times each day, but Muslims also pray to Allah at other times in their own words. All prayers must be from the heart.

10. Is it true that only men go to the mosque for worship?

    No. Men are expected to go to the mosque but women are allowed, although they pray in separate areas from men, for reasons of modesty and purity.

11. When Muslims pray five times each day, how long is each prayer time?

    The length varies during each of the five prayer times, but one can count on praying at least one hour every day.

12. What do Muslims do if they are traveling in a car or airplane at a time for prayer?

    There are complex rules about how Muslims are to pray during travel. It depends on who they are with, what prayer time is involved, and whether travel can be interrupted.

13. Where and when do women worship?

    Women are to pray five times per day, just like men. They usually worship at home.

14. Women in traditional Muslim countries are often fully veiled in public. Why are Muslim women in the United States usually not veiled that way?

    Veiling customs vary in Muslim countries and also in the United States. There are some American Muslim groups that demand total veiling, but most Muslim women in the United States have adopted a more relaxed public dress code based on the Islamic teaching they follow.

15. Are non-Arab Muslims considered second-class citizens in Islam?

    Though Islam teaches that all Muslims are equal, non-Arab

Muslims are sometimes treated as second-class citizens in Saudi Arabia or other parts of the Middle East.

16. Do Muslims say grace before meals?

Muslims are to thank Allah for food and drink both before and after meals.

17. Is there a specific age at which boys begin to participate at the mosque?

No. This varies, but Muslim leaders encourage parents to teach their children the daily prayers as early as the age of two.

18. Does the imam perform the same functions as a Christian pastor?

Generally, the Muslim imam performs the same functions as the Christian pastor: teaching, leading in prayer, counseling, and giving advice. The imam's role differs mainly in helping Muslims to apply the details of Islamic law.

19. In what areas of the world is Islam growing today?

Islam is growing rapidly in the United States, especially among African Americans, and in southern Europe. Throughout the twentieth century Islam grew significantly in the sub-Saharan areas of Africa.

20. What is the biggest challenge facing Islam today?

The leaders of Islam must address the issue of personal freedom under Islamic rule. As well, Muslims must now decide what response they will make to militant, extremist versions of the faith.

Bibliography and Additional Resources

General

Ayaan Hirsi Ali. *Infidel* (New York: Free Press, 2007).

Paul M. Barrett. *American Islam* (New York: Farrar, Straus and Giroux, 2007).

Bruce Bawer. *Surrender* (New York: Doubleday, 2009).

James A. Beverley. *Christ and Islam* (Joplin: College Press, 2001, 2nd ed.).

_____. *Islamic Faith in America* (New York: Facts on File, 2011, 2nd ed.).

_____. *Nelson's Illustrated Guide to Religions* (Nashville: Nelson, 2009).

Gary Bunt. *iMuslims: Rewiring the House of Islam* (Chapel Hill: University of North Carolina Press, 2009).

George W. Braswell Jr. *Islam* (Nashville: Broadman & Holman, 1996).

David Cook. *Contemporary Muslim Apocalyptic Literature* (Syracuse: Syracuse UP, 2005).

_____. *Studies in Islamic Apocalyptic* (Princeton: Darwin Press, 2002).

Kenneth Cragg. *The Call of the Minaret* (Maryknoll: Orbis, 1985).

John Esposito and Dalia Mogahed. *Who Speaks for Islam?* (New York: Oxford, 2008).

_____ and Ibrahim Kalin, eds. *The 500 Most Influential Muslims in the World* (Amman: Royal Islamic Strategic Studies Centre, 2009).

Jean-Pierre Filiu. *Apocalypse in Islam* (Los Angeles: University of California, 2011).

Robert Fisk. *The Great War for Civilization* (New York: Knopf, 2005).

Norman Geisler and Abdul Saleed. *Answering Islam* (Grand Rapids: Baker, 1993).

Samuel Huntington. *The Clash of Civilizations* (New York: Simon & Schuster, 1996).

Efraim Karsh, *Islamic Imperialism* (New Haven: Yale University Press, 2006).

Martin Kramer. *Ivory Towers in the Sand* (Washington: Washington Institute for
    Near East Policy, 2001).
Charles Kurzman, ed. *Liberal Islam* (Oxford: Oxford University Press, 1998).
Hans Küng. *Islam* (London: Oneworld, 2007).
Bernard Lewis. *Islam and the West* (New York: Oxford, 1993).
Rick Love. *Muslims, Magic and the Kingdom of God* (Pasadena: William Carey,
    2001).
Irshad Manji. *The Trouble with Islam Today* (New York: Vintage, 2005).
Paul Marshall, ed. *Religious Freedom in the World* (Nashville: Broadman & Hol-
    man, 2000).
Jane Dammen McAuliffe, ed. *The Cambridge Companion to the Qur'an* (Cambridge:
    Cambridge University Press, 2006).
V. S. Naipaul, *Among the Believers* (London: Penguin, 1982).
Seyyed Nasr, ed., *Islamic Spirituality: Manifestations* (New York: Crossroad Pub-
    lishing Company, 1991).
Vali Nasr. *The Shia Revival* (New York: Norton, 2006).
Michael Oren. *Power, Faith and Fantasy* (New York: Norton, 2007).
Melanie Phillips. *Londonistan* (New York: Encounter, 2006).
Fazlur Rahman. *Islam* (Chicago: University of Chicago Press, 1979).
Andrew Rippin. *Muslims* (London: Routledge, 2000).
Reinhard Schulze. *A Modern History of the Islamic World* (New York: New York
    University Press, 2000).
Mark Sedgwick. *Islam and Muslims* (Boston: Intercultural Press, 2006).
_____. *Sufism: The Essentials* (Cairo: AUC Press, 2003).
Jane I. Smith. *Islam in America* (West Sussex: Columbia, 1999).
Christopher Tyerman. *God's War: A New History of the Crusades* (Cambridge:
    Harvard, 2006).
Josef Van Ess. *The Flowering of Muslim Theology* (Cambridge: Harvard University
    Press, 2006).
Ibn Warraq. *Why I Am Not a Muslim* (Amherst: Prometheus, 1995).

Muhammad

Clinton Bennett. *In Search of Muhammad* (London: Continuum, 1998).
Michael Cook. *Muhammad* (Oxford: Oxford University Press, 1983).
Martin Lings. *Muhammad* (Rochester: Inner Traditions, 1983).
Harald Motzki, ed. *The Biography of Muhammad: The Issue of the Sources* (Boston:
    E.J. Brill, 2000).

F. E. Peters. *Muhammad and the Origins of Islam* (Herndon: State University of New York Press, 1994).

Tariq Ramadan. *In the Footsteps of the Prophet* (Oxford: Oxford University Press, 2007).

Maxime Rodinson. *Muhammad*, trans. Anne Carter (London: Penguin, 1976).

Uri Rubin, ed. *The Life of Muhammad* (London: Ashgate, 1998).

Annemarie Schimmel. *And Muhammad is His Messenger* (Chapel Hill: University of North Carolina Press, 1985).

W. Montgomery Watt. *Muhammad: Prophet and Statesman* (Oxford: Oxford University Press, 1961).

Women and Islam

Geraldine Brooks. *Nine Parts of Desire* (London: Penguin, 1996).

Elizabeth Warnock Fernea. *In Search of Islamic Feminism: One Woman's Global Journey* (New York: Anchor, 1998).

Jan Goodwin. *Price of Honor* (New York: Little, Brown, & Co., 1994).

Fatima Mernissi. *The Veil and the Male Elite* (Boston: Addison-Wesley, 1991).

Anne Sofie Roald. *Women in Islam* (London: Routledge, 2001).

Israel and the Palestinian issue

Mitchell Bard. *Myths and Facts* (Chevy Chase, MD: AICE, 2002).

Thomas Friedman. *From Beirut to Jerusalem* (New York: Farrar Straus & Giroux, 1989).

David Grossman. *The Yellow Wind* (New York: Farrar Straus & Giroux, 1988).

Efraim Karsh. *Fabricating Israeli History* (Portland: Frank Cass, 2000, rev. ed.).

Efraim and Inari Karsh. *Empires of the Sand* (Cambridge: Harvard University Press, 1999).

Walter Laqueur and Barry Rubin, eds. *The Israel-Arab Reader* (New York: Penguin, 2001).

Benny Morris. *Righteous Victims* (New York: Vintage, 2001).

Michael Oren. *Six Days of War* (Oxford: Oxford University Press, 2002).

Ilan Pappe. *The Ethnic Cleansing of Palestine* (Oxford: Oneworld, 2006).

Eugene L. Rogan and Avi Shlaim, eds. *The War for Palestine* (Cambridge: Cambridge University Press, 2001).

Dennis Ross. *The Missing Peace* (New York: Farrar, Straus and Giroux, 2004).

Tom Segev. *One Palestine, Complete* (New York: Henry Holt/Metropolitan Books, 2000).

Avi Shlaim. *The Iron Wall* (New York: W.W. Norton, 2001).

Jihad, Terrorism, Middle East, and the West

Peter L. Bergen. *Holy War Inc.* (New York: Free Press, 2001).

Michael Bonner. *Jihad in Islamic History* (Princeton, NJ: Princeton University Press, 2006).

Ian Buruma. *Murder in Amsterdam* (New York: Penguin, 2006).

David Cole. *The Torture Memos* (New York: The New Press, 2009).

Steve Coll. *Ghost Wars* (New York: Penguin, 2004).

_____. *The Bin Ladens* (New York: Penguin, 2008).

Steven Emerson. *Jihad Incorporated* (Amherst: Prometheus, 2006).

Daveed Gartenstein-Ross. *My Year Inside Radical Islam* (New York: Tarcher/Penguin, 2007).

Bruce Hoffman. *Inside Terrorism* (New York: Columbia University Press, 2006, rev. ed.).

Roland Jacquard. *In the Name of Osama bin Laden* (Durham: Duke University Press, 2002).

John Kelsay. *Arguing the Just War in Islam* (Cambridge, Mass.: Harvard University Press, 2007).

Gilles Kepel and Jean-Pierre Milelli, eds. *Al Qaeda in its Own Words*, trans. Pascale Ghazaleh (Cambridge: Harvard University Press, 2008).

Kanan Makiya. *Cruelty and Silence* (New York: W. W. Norton, 1993).

Monte and Princess Palmer. *At the Heart of Terror: Islam, Jihadists, and America's War on Terrorism* (Lanham, MD: Rowman & Littlefield, 2004).

Walid Phares. *The Confrontation* (Basingstoke: Macmillan Palgrave, 2008).

Daniel Pipes. *Militant Islam Reaches America* (New York: W.W. Norton, 2003).

Ahmed Rashid. *Taliban* (New Haven: Yale University Press, 2001).

_____. *Descent into Chaos* (New York: Viking, 2008).

Thomas Ricks. *Fiasco* (New York: Penguin, 2006).

Michael Scheuer. *Marching Toward Hell* (New York: Free Press, 2008).

Stephen Schwartz. *The Two Faces of Islam* (New York: Doubleday, 2002).

Jessica Stern. *Terror in the Name of God* (New York: Harper, 2004).

Bob Woodward. *State of Denial* (New York: Simon & Schuster, 2006).

Lawrence Wright. *The Looming Tower* (New York: Knopf, 2006).

Internet and Electronic Resources

Christian Sites

Answering Islam
www.answering-islam.org

Joseph Cumming (Yale)
www.josephcumming.com

Frontiers
www.frontiers.org

Carl Medearis
www.carlmedearis.com

Muslim-Christian Debate Web site (features work of Jay Smith):
www.debate.org.uk

Peace Catalyst International (Rick Love)
www.ricklove.net

Quran and Injil (Gordon Nickel)
www.quranandinjil.org

World Evangelical Alliance Peace and Reconciliation Initiative
www.weapri.org

Yale Center for Faith and Culture (Joseph Cumming)
www.yale.edu/faith/rp/rp.htm

Academic Sites

Abu Dhabi Gallup Center
www.abudhabigallupcenter.com/home.aspx

Gary Bunt
www.virtuallyislamic.com

Carl W. Ernst (University of North Carolina)
www.unc.edu/~cernst/index.html

Gallup Center for Muslim Studies
www.gallup.com/se/127907/Gallup-Center-Muslim-Studies.aspx

Alan Godlas (University of Georgia)
www.uga.edu/islam

Islamic Law Info
www.llrx.com/features/islamiclaw.htm (Andrew Grossman)
www.jus.uio.no/lm/islamic.law/islamic.law.html (Ralph Amissa)

Martin Kramer
www.martinkramer.org

Liberal Islam (Charles Kurzman)
www.unc.edu/~kurzman/LiberalIslamLinks.htm

Muslim Sexual Ethics Links
www.brandeis.edu/projects/fse/muslim/mus-web.html

Daniel Pipes
www.danielpipes.org

Muslim Sites

A Common Word (Reconciliation Program)
www.acommonword.com

Al-Muhaddith (download site for Qur'an, hadith, Islamic legal material):
www.muhaddith.org

Fethullah Gulen (Turkish intellectual)
www.fethullahgulen.org

Amr Khaled (Egyptian preacher)
amrkhaled.net

Irshad Manji (liberal feminist Muslim)
www.irshadmanji.com

IslamiCity
www.islam.org

Islamweb
www.islamweb.net

Mamalist of Islamic Links
www.jannah.org/mamalist

Mona Eltahawy (columnist)
www.monaeltahawy.com

Musawah (Muslim family equality)
www.musawah.org

Israel-Palestinian Conflict

Academic Info Middle East
www.academicinfo.net/mestpeace.html

Aljazeera
www.aljazeera.com

The American Israel Public Affairs Committee
www.aipac.org

Bitterlemons
www.bitterlemons.net

Brookings Institution
www.brookings.edu

Churches for Middle East Peace
www.cmep.org

The Committee for Accuracy in Middle East Reporting in America
www.camera.org

Council on Foreign Relations
www.cfr.org

The Electronic Intifada
www.electronicintifada.net

Ha'aretz
www.haaretzdaily.com

Israel Government Gateway
www.gov.il/firstgov/english

Jerusalem Post
www.jpost.com

The Jewish Virtual Library
www.us-israel.org/jsource/index.html

Jewish World Review
www.jewishworldreview.com

Media Watch International
www.honestreporting.com

Middle East Forum
www.meforum.org

Middle East Media Research Institute
www.memri.org

Tikkun
www.tikkun.org

Washington Institute for Near East Policy
www.washingtoninstitute.org

Washington Report on Middle East Affairs
www.wrmea.com

Ex-Muslim Sites

www.faithfreedom.org

www.apostatesofislam.com

Terrorism/Militant Islam

Afghanistan Analyst (Christopher Bleuer)
afghanistan-analyst.org

All Things Counter Terrorism (Leah Farrall)
allthingscounterterrorism.com

Bruce Bawer
www.brucebawer.com

Jarret Brachman
jarretbrachman.net

Combating Terrorism Center (West Point)
www.ctc.usma.edu

Counterterrorism Blog
counterterrorismblog.org

Douglas Farah
www.douglasfarah.com

FBI Counterterrorism
www.fbi.gov/about-us/investigate/terrorism/terrorism

Foundation for Defense of Democracies
defenddemocracy.org

ICT – Terrorism and Counter-Terrorism
www.ict.org.il

Investigative Project on Terrorism (Steven Emerson)
www.investigativeproject.org

Jamestown Foundation
www.jamestown.org

Jihad Watch
www.jihadwatch.org

Jihadica
www.jihadica.com

Jihadology (Aaron Zelin)
jihadology.net

Online Jihad
online-jihad.com

Daniel Pipes
www.danielpipes.org

U.S. State Department
www.state.gov/s/ct

CD Christian Resource

J. Dudley Woodberry, ed. *The World of Islam 2.0*. (Colorado Springs: Global Mapping International).